NYSTCE 074 CST
Library & Media Specialist
Teacher Certification Exam

By: Sharon Wynne, M.S.
Southern Connecticut State University

"And, while there's no reason yet to panic, I think it's only prudent that we make preparations to panic."

XAMonline, INC.
Boston

Copyright © 2007 XAMonline, Inc.
All rights reserved. No part of the material protected by this copyright notice may be reproduced or utilized in any form or by any means, electronic or mechanical, including photocopying, recording or by any information storage and retrievable system, without written permission from the copyright holder.

To obtain permission(s) to use the material from this work for any purpose including workshops or seminars, please submit a written request to:

XAMonline, Inc.
21 Orient Ave.
Melrose, MA 02176
Toll Free 1-800-509-4128
Email: info@xamonline.com
Web www.xamonline.com
Fax: 1-781-662-9268

Library of Congress Cataloging-in-Publication Data originally

Wynne, Sharon A.
    CST Library & Media Specialist 074: Teacher Certification / Sharon A. Wynne. - 2nd ed. ISBN 978-1-58197-863-6
    1. CST Library & Media Specialist 074.   2. Study Guides.
    3. NYSTCE   4. Teachers' Certification & Licensure.   5. Careers

Disclaimer:
The opinions expressed in this publication are the sole works of XAMonline and were created independently from the National Education Association, Educational Testing Service, or any State Department of Education, National Evaluation Systems or other testing affiliates.

Between the time of publication and printing, state specific standards as well as testing formats and website information may change that is not included in part or in whole within this product. Sample test questions are developed by XAMonline and reflect similar content as on real tests; however, they are not former tests. XAMonline assembles content that aligns with state standards but makes no claims nor guarantees teacher candidates a passing score. Numerical scores are determined by testing companies such as NES or ETS and then are compared with individual state standards. A passing score varies from state to state.

Printed in the United States of America   œ-1

NYSTCE: CST Library & Media Specialist 074
ISBN: 1-58197-863-6

TEACHER CERTIFICATION STUDY GUIDE

Table of Contents

pg.

SUBAREA I.   **THE LIBRARY MEDIA PROGRAM**

COMPETENCY 0001 UNDERSTAND THE ROLE OF THE LIBRARY MEDIA PROGRAM AND ITS RELATIONSHIP TO THE TOTAL SCHOOL PROGRAM 1

Skill 1.1   Demonstrating understanding of the importance of creating an environment that supports the multiple uses of the library media center and promotes lifelong learning... 1

Skill 1.2   Aligning library media program goals and objectives with curricular needs and identifying appropriate library media resources, personnel, and services to support the curriculum (e.g., addressing the needs of the learning community with regard to resources-based learning, information literacy skills and strategies, and resources in the curriculum) 1

Skill 1.3   Recognizing the integral and collaborative role of the library media program in all curricular areas 2

Skill 1.4   Identifying characteristics and functions of an effective school library media program.. 2

Skill 1.5   Formulating a mission statement for the library media program that reflects overall school and district goals and objectives 3

Skill 1.6   Recognizing the role of the library media program in providing equitable physical and intellectual access to information, ideas, and learning and teaching tools.. 4

COMPETENCY 0002 UNDERSTAND THE ROLES AND RESPONSIBILITIES OF THE LIBRARY MEDIA SPECIALIST......................... 5

Skill 2.1   Applying strategies for creating a positive teaching and learning climate in the library media center 5

Skill 2.2   Applying strategies for encouraging students to take responsibility for their own learning 5

Skill 2.3   Demonstrating knowledge of the management functions of library media specialists with regard to services, facilities, personnel, and funding... 6

Skill 2.4   Recognizing the importance of building and maintaining collaborative partnerships to support the library media program 7

TEACHER CERTIFICATION STUDY GUIDE

Skill 2.5 Recognizing the role of the library media specialist in providing expertise and advocacy in collection development and the use of information technology and resources 7

COMPETENCY 0003 UNDERSTAND THE INSTRUCTIONAL PARTNER ROLE OF THE LIBRARY MEDIA SPECIALIST IN CURRICULUM DEVELOPMENT 8

Skill 3.1 Demonstrating knowledge of basic principles of curriculum development and standardized practices 8

Skill 3.2 Demonstrating knowledge of methods for integrating New York State Learning Standards and national information literacy standards into the school curriculum 8

Skill 3.3 Identifying types and characteristics of various instructional materials and resources (e.g., overhead transparencies, multimedia presentations) 9

Skill 3.4 Examining considerations related to the design and production of instructional materials (e.g., intended audience) and applying procedures for producing and reproducing various types of instructional materials 10

Skill 3.5 Demonstrating knowledge of methods for sharing information with faculty and staff for professional enrichment 12

COMPETENCY 0004 UNDERSTAND PROFESSIONAL STANDARDS, LEGAL REQUIREMENTS, AND ETHICAL ISSUES IN THE LIBRARY MEDIA PROGRAM 13

Skill 4.1 Identifying professional responsibilities of the library media specialist (e.g., ensuring equitable access to information, instructing and training other members of the learning community about library media resources and their uses, serving as an advocate for students and the library media program, recognizing and addressing issues of bias and diversity) 13

Skill 4.2 Demonstrating knowledge of ethical responsibilities of library media personnel in various situations 13

Skill 4.3 Applying professional and legal standards and guidelines in various library media contexts... 14

Skill 4.4 Demonstrating knowledge of issues related to copyright and intellectual property and of legislation affecting library media programs 16

TEACHER CERTIFICATION STUDY GUIDE

SUBAREA II.   **LIBRARY MEDIA RESOURCES**

COMPETENCY 0005 UNDERSTAND THE RELATIONSHIP BETWEEN THE LIBRARY MEDIA PROGRAM AND INFORMATION RESOURCES AND SERVICES BEYOND THE SCHOOL 19

Skill 5.1   Demonstrating understanding of the role of libraries in a democratic society to sustain lifelong learning 19

Skill 5.2   Recognizing the role of the library media program in connecting teachers and students to local, district, state, national, and global resources 19

Skill 5.3   Demonstrating knowledge of the characteristics and uses of Information resources and services beyond the school (e.g., electronic services, public libraries, interlibrary loan, state service providers for special populations) 20

COMPETENCY 0006 UNDERSTAND TYPES AND CHARACTERISTICS OF PRINT, NONPRINT, AND ELECTRONIC RESOURCES 22

Skill 6.1   Demonstrating knowledge of types, characteristics, and uses of print resources 22

Skill 6.2   Demonstrating knowledge of types, characteristics, and uses of nonprint resources 22

Skill 6.3   Recognizing and comparing advantages and limitations of various resources and Formats 23

COMPETENCY 0007 UNDERSTAND TYPES AND CHARACTERISTICS OF LITERATURE FOR CHILDREN AND YOUNG ADULTS 24

Skill 7.1   Demonstrating knowledge of various forms and genres of literature (e.g., biography, poetry, drama, science fiction) 24

Skill 7.2   Identifying characteristics of literature for children and young adults 25

Skill 7.3   Recognizing developmental factors that should be considered when selecting literature for individual students 25

Skill 7.4   Applying strategies and activities that promote the appreciation and enjoyment of reading 26

COMPETENCY 0008 UNDERSTAND ISSUES AND PROCEDURES RELATED TO COLLECTION DEVELOPMENT 27

Skill 8.1 Identifying sources for the acquisition of materials and equipment for the library media program 27

Skill 8.2 Developing and applying criteria for evaluating and selecting resources and equipment that will enable the library media program to support the school's mission and objectives 29

Skill 8.3 Applying procedures for working collaboratively with others to identify the needs of students; plan purchases; and design, develop, and evaluate resources 35

Skill 8.4 Applying procedures for communicating with and involving the learning community in the evaluation, selection, and deselection processes 36

Skill 8.5 Analyzing issues and considerations related to the selection of Resources and equipment for a school library media program (e.g., intellectual freedom, copyright, specialized collection development, accessibility, avoidance of bias) and using professional selection tools 37

Skill 8.6 Demonstrating knowledge of considerations involved in collection analysis (e.g., balance, alignment with curriculum and learning standards, representation of diversity, age of collection) 38

SUBAREA III.   INFORMATION LITERACY SKILLS

COMPETENCY 0009 UNDERSTAND METHODS FOR TEACHING INFORMATION LITERACY SKILLS TO STUDENTS 39

Skill 9.1 Using knowledge of child development principles and educational pedagogy to provide students with age-appropriate information sources and instructional strategies and services 39

Skill 9.2 Demonstrating understanding of various approaches to an information-seeking process 39

Skill 9.3 Evaluating differentiated teaching strategies for encouraging critical and creative thinking and developing information literacy skills (e.g., reading skills, listening skills, viewing skills) 40

Skill 9.4 Selecting and adapting strategies and resources, including new and adaptive technologies, to assist students with diverse learning abilities, styles, and needs 41

Skill 9.5	Recognizing ways to assist students seeking information for personal interest and self-improvement and to promote independent learning opportunities that address various learning styles	41
Skill 9.6	Demonstrating knowledge of national information literacy standards and guidelines	42

COMPETENCY 0010 UNDERSTAND HOW TO DETERMINE INFORMATION NEEDS AND INITIATE SEARCHES AND HOW TO TEACH THESE SKILLS TO STUDENTS 43

Skill 10.1	Applying procedures for formulating essential questions or problems and designing information search plans	43
Skill 10.2	Evaluating potential sources of information with regard to specific criteria (e.g., currency, format, authority, accuracy, bias, coverage)	43
Skill 10.3	Recognizing ways of structuring searches across a variety of sources and formats to locate the best information for a particular need	44
Skill 10.4	Applying strategies for eliciting information needs from learners (e.g., identifying the type of information needed, placing information needs in a frame of reference, relating the information to prior knowledge)	45

COMPETENCY 0011 UNDERSTAND HOW TO LOCATE AND ACCESS RESOURCES AND HOW TO TEACH THESE SKILLS TO STUDENTS 46

Skill 11.1	Identifying key words, subject headings, and cross-references for searches	46
Skill 11.2	Applying procedures for accessing information from diverse sources within and outside the library media center	46
Skill 11.3	Demonstrating knowledge of strategies for conducting electronic searches (e.g., identifying electronic sources, restricting a search using Boolean operators)	47
Skill 11.4	Recognizing ways of helping students develop skills and independence in locating and accessing resources	47

TEACHER CERTIFICATION STUDY GUIDE

COMPETENCY 0012 UNDERSTAND STRATEGIES FOR ASSESSING PROGRESS DURING A SEARCH, ANALYZING AND EVALUATING INFORMATION, AND TEACHING THESE SKILLS TO STUDENTS 48

Skill 12.1 Recognizing ways of evaluating the progress of a search 48

Skill 12.2 Determining appropriate adjustments to search strategies and evaluating whether expected outcomes of a search were achieved 48

Skill 12.3 Applying criteria for evaluating information (e.g., determining authority, distinguishing fact from opinion, comparing information from different sources) 49

Skill 12.4 Evaluating the effectiveness of information presented in various Formats 49

Skill 12.5 Applying skills for summarizing, organizing, and synthesizing Information 49

Skill 12.6 Applying methods of helping students evaluate and interpret information (e.g., determining whether information addresses the original problem, drawing conclusions from information obtained in a search) 50

COMPETENCY 0013 UNDERSTAND HOW TO COMMUNICATE INFORMATION OBTAINED FROM A SEARCH AND HOW TO TEACH THIS SKILL TO STUDENTS 51

Skill 13.1 Applying guidelines for preparing a bibliography or works-cited list 51

Skill 13.2 Organizing information into a form that clearly communicates what has been learned 51

Skill 13.3 Applying procedures for selecting an appropriate format to communicate information (e.g., print, audio, video, multimedia) and for producing an effective end product 53

Skill 13.4 Applying methods for helping students think creatively about approaches to and formats for communicating information 53

LIBRARY & MEDIA SPECIALIST

TEACHER CERTIFICATION STUDY GUIDE

SUBAREA IV. PROGRAM ADMINISTRATION AND LEADERSHIP

COMPETENCY 0014 UNDERSTAND THE LEADERSHIP ROLE OF THE LIBRARY MEDIA SPECIALIST WITHIN THE ENTIRE EDUCATIONAL COMMUNITY 54

Skill 14.1 Applying strategies for participating in district, building, department, and grade level curriculum design and assessment projects to ensure that the library media program is integral to the school curriculum 54

Skill 14.2 Applying advocacy strategies to build support for the library media program among teachers, administrators, school board members, parents/guardians, students, and the community 55

Skill 14.3 Applying procedures for establishing partnerships with the school community to support learning objectives, share the vision of the library media program, and engage in long-range, strategic planning 55

Skill 14.4 Demonstrating knowledge of ways to incorporate the library media program in educational reform 56

COMPETENCY 0015 UNDERSTAND FACILITIES USE IN THE LIBRARY MEDIA CENTER 58

Skill 15.1 Analyzing factors to be considered when designing and furnishing a library media center (e.g., efficient use of space; areas needed for specific purposes; age appropriateness; providing accommodations for technology and for students with special developmental and educational needs; creating a warm, friendly atmosphere that is conducive to learning) 58

Skill 15.2 Identifying, evaluating, establishing, and using delivery systems to retrieve information in all formats and for all ability levels 61

Skill 15.3 Demonstrating knowledge of scheduling considerations and applying techniques for scheduling library media center resources, equipment, and space (e.g., flexible scheduling) 62

Skill 15.4 Applying procedures for operating, storing, maintaining, inventorying, and securing library media resources 63

Skill 15.5 Recognizing policies that promote equitable access to and use of library media Facilities 64

COMPETENCY 0016 UNDERSTAND PROCEDURES FOR LIBRARY MEDIA RESOURCE ORGANIZATION AND CIRCULATION ... 65

Skill 16.1 Identifying and applying standard methods of classifying and cataloging library media materials (e.g., Dewey Decimal System, Sears List of Subject Headings, U.S. MARC, AACR2, ALA filing rules) 65

Skill 16.2 Demonstrating knowledge of collection management principles and Procedures 66

Skill 16.3 Recognizing types of circulation patterns, controls, records, and systems and analyzing factors to be considered when establishing use and circulation policies 68

Skill 16.4 Evaluating and implementing policies to ensure equitable and reasonable access to library resources 69

COMPETENCY 0017 UNDERSTAND PROCEDURES AND ISSUES RELATED TO FISCAL AND STAFF MANAGEMENT IN LIBRARY MEDIA PROGRAMS 70

Skill 17.1 Determining fiscal needs, setting fiscal goals, and establishing fiscal priorities for the library media program 70

Skill 17.2 Applying strategies for communicating effectively within and outside the learning community about the status and needs of the library media program 70

Skill 17.3 Applying procedures for preparing budgets and reports, maintaining records, and running a library media program within budget 71

Skill 17.4 Demonstrating basic knowledge of local, state, federal, and private sources of funding for library media programs 73

Skill 17.5 Applying principles and procedures for selecting, supervising, and evaluating staff and for handling personnel and staffing issues 74

Skill 17.6 Recognizing characteristics, roles, and training needs associated with library media personnel and applying methods for conducting professional development activities for library media staff 75

TEACHER CERTIFICATION STUDY GUIDE

COMPETENCY 0018............................UNDERSTAND THE DEVELOPMENT, IMPLEMENTATION, AND ONGOING EVALUATION OF A LIBRARY MEDIA PROGRAM..................................77

Skill 18.1 Using a needs assessment to establish program goals and to identify appropriate activities and resources to meet those goals 77

Skill 18.2 Recognizing ways of involving the learning community in the formulation and communication of a long-range plan for the library media program (e.g., establishing a school library media planning team) 78

Skill 18.3 Applying procedures for evaluating the effectiveness of a library mediaprogram (e.g., with regard to collection, facility, personnel, etc.) 80

Sample Test..82

Answer Key 104

Rigor Table 105

Rationales..106

TEACHER CERTIFICATION STUDY GUIDE

Great Study and Testing Tips!

What to study in order to prepare for the subject assessments is the focus of this study guide but equally important is *how* you study.

You can increase your chances of truly mastering the information by taking some simple, but effective steps.

Study Tips:

1. Some foods aid the learning process. Foods such as milk, nuts, seeds, rice, and oats help your study efforts by releasing natural memory enhancers called CCKs (*cholecystokinin*) composed of *tryptophan*, *choline*, and *phenylalanine*. All of these chemicals enhance the neurotransmitters associated with memory. Before studying, try a light, protein-rich meal of eggs, turkey, and fish. All of these foods release the memory enhancing chemicals. The better the connections, the more you comprehend.

Likewise, before you take a test, stick to a light snack of energy boosting and relaxing foods. A glass of milk, a piece of fruit, or some peanuts all release various memory-boosting chemicals and help you to relax and focus on the subject at hand.

2. Learn to take great notes. A by-product of our modern culture is that we have grown accustomed to getting our information in short doses (i.e. TV news sound bites or USA Today style newspaper articles.)

Consequently, we've subconsciously trained ourselves to assimilate information better in neat little packages. If your notes are scrawled all over the paper, it fragments the flow of the information. Strive for clarity. Newspapers use a standard format to achieve clarity. Your notes can be much clearer through use of proper formatting. A very effective format is called the *"Cornell Method."*

> Take a sheet of loose-leaf lined notebook paper and draw a line all the way down the paper about 1-2" from the left-hand edge.
>
> Draw another line across the width of the paper about 1-2" up from the bottom. Repeat this process on the reverse side of the page.

Look at the highly effective result. You have ample room for notes, a left hand margin for special emphasis items or inserting supplementary data from the textbook, a large area at the bottom for a brief summary, and a little rectangular space for just about anything you want.

3. Get the concept then the details. Too often we focus on the details and don't gather an understanding of the concept. However, if you simply memorize only dates, places, or names, you may well miss the whole point of the subject.

A key way to understand things is to put them in your own words. If you are working from a textbook, automatically summarize each paragraph in your mind. If you are outlining text, don't simply copy the author's words.

Rephrase them in your own words. You remember your own thoughts and words much better than someone else's, and subconsciously tend to associate the important details to the core concepts.

4. Ask Why? Pull apart written material paragraph by paragraph and don't forget the captions under the illustrations.

Example: If the heading is "Stream Erosion", flip it around to read "Why do streams erode?" Then answer the questions.

If you train your mind to think in a series of questions and answers, not only will you learn more, but it also helps to lessen the test anxiety because you are used to answering questions.

5. Read for reinforcement and future needs. Even if you only have 10 minutes, put your notes or a book in your hand. Your mind is similar to a computer; you have to input data in order to have it processed. *By reading, you are creating the neural connections for future retrieval.* The more times you read something, the more you reinforce the learning of ideas.

Even if you don't fully understand something on the first pass, *your mind stores much of the material for later recall.*

6. Relax to learn so go into exile. Our bodies respond to an inner clock called biorhythms. Burning the midnight oil works well for some people, but not everyone.

If possible, set aside a particular place to study that is free of distractions. Shut off the television, cell phone, and pager and exile your friends and family during your study period.

If you really are bothered by silence, try background music. Light classical music at a low volume has been shown to aid in concentration over other types. Music that evokes pleasant emotions without lyrics is highly suggested. Try just about anything by Mozart. It relaxes you.

7. Use arrows not highlighters. At best, it's difficult to read a page full of yellow, pink, blue, and green streaks. Try staring at a neon sign for a while and you'll soon see that the horde of colors obscure the message.

A quick note, a brief dash of color, an underline, and an arrow pointing to a particular passage is much clearer than a horde of highlighted words.

8. Budget your study time. Although you shouldn't ignore any of the material, *allocate your available study time in the same ratio that topics may appear on the test.*

TEACHER CERTIFICATION STUDY GUIDE

Testing Tips:

1. <u>Get smart, play dumb</u>. Don't read anything into the question. Don't make an assumption that the test writer is looking for something else than what is asked. Stick to the question as written and don't read extra things into it.

2. <u>Read the question and all the choices *twice* before answering the question</u>. You may miss something by not carefully reading, and then re-reading both the question and the answers.

If you really don't have a clue as to the right answer, leave it blank on the first time through. Go on to the other questions, as they may provide a clue as to how to answer the skipped questions.

If later on, you still can't answer the skipped ones . . . **Guess.** The only penalty for guessing is that you *might* get it wrong. Only one thing is certain; if you don't put anything down, you will get it wrong!

3. <u>Turn the question into a statement</u>. Look at the way the questions are worded. The syntax of the question usually provides a clue. Does it seem more familiar as a statement rather than as a question? Does it sound strange?

By turning a question into a statement, you may be able to spot if an answer sounds right, and it may also trigger memories of material you have read.

4. <u>Look for hidden clues</u>. It's actually very difficult to compose multiple-foil (choice) questions without giving away part of the answer in the options presented.

In most multiple-choice questions you can often readily eliminate one or two of the potential answers. This leaves you with only two real possibilities and automatically your odds go to Fifty-Fifty for very little work.

5. <u>Trust your instincts</u>. For every fact that you have read, you subconsciously retain something of that knowledge. On questions that you aren't really certain about, go with your basic instincts. **Your first impression on how to answer a question is usually correct.**

6. <u>Mark your answers directly on the test booklet</u>. Don't bother trying to fill in the optical scan sheet on the first pass through the test.

7. <u>Watch the clock</u>! You have a set amount of time to answer the questions. Don't get bogged down trying to answer a single question at the expense of 10 questions you can more readily answer.

LIBRARY & MEDIA SPECIALIST

THIS PAGE BLANK

TEACHER CERTIFICATION STUDY GUIDE

SUBAREA I. THE LIBRARY MEDIA PROGRAM

COMPETENCY 0001 UNDERSTAND THE ROLE OF THE LIBRARY MEDIA PROGRAM AND ITS RELATIONSHIP TO THE TOTAL SCHOOL PROGRAM

Skill 1.1 Demonstrating understanding of the importance of creating an environment that supports the multiple uses of the library media center and promotes lifelong learning

A student-centered media center begins by providing access to resources in an environment that is both interesting and inviting. The space should be well-organized and clearly labeled so that resources can be located. It should have a welcoming atmosphere that entices students and staff to come to the media center to learn.

The school library media specialist is crucial to the development of a climate that encourages learning. To provide such as atmosphere the school library media specialist must be willing to:

- promote the program as a wonderful place for learning
- arrange materials so that they are easy to locate
- set flexible schedules that allow for just-in-time learning
- be eager to work with students and staff
- maintain an attractive and inviting space
- collaborate with school staff and students

Skill 1.2 Aligning library media program goals and objectives with curricular needs and identifying appropriate library media resources, personnel, and services to support the curriculum (e.g. addressing the needs of the learning community with regard to resources-based learning, information literacy skills and strategies, and resources in the curriculum)

An effective school library media program facilitates the integration of information skills into core content areas. The school library media specialist plays a crucial role in the effective functioning of the program. The more the media specialists understands the needs of the population they serve, the more closely the media program will reflect the learning goals of the school

Through collaboration with classroom teachers, media specialists can gain insight to curricular needs, promote information literacy, and become recognized as partners in the educational process. There are steps a media specialist can take to facilitate this process.

- Develop a working knowledge of the curriculum used within the school.

- Participate in grade-level, school-district and state curriculum planning efforts.
- Collaborate with teachers to identify the resources needed to support the curriculum.
- Collaborate with teachers to integrate information skills into the curriculum.

Skill 1.3 Recognizing the integral and collaborative role of the library media program in all curricular areas

One of the single most important parts of a successful school library media program is collaboration between the school library media specialist and classroom teachers.

To support the collaborative process there are key skills the media specialist must possess. These include:

- **Flexibility:** The ability to adjust to the differing needs of staff and students and flexibility with time.
- **Curriculum Expertise:** Knowledge of the curriculum being taught at the grade levels being served. This makes the media specialist an invaluable partner.
- **Leadership:** Setting the path in which the media program should move, setting goals and expectations, serving as advocate for the teachers as well as the media program.
- **Approachability:** Establishing good rapport with staff and students and being someone they know will be willing to go above and beyond the call of duty.
- **Persistence:** Keeping going and keeping the media program moving forward.

Skill 1.4 Identifying characteristics and functions of an effective school library media program

An effective school library media program can become the heart of learning in any school environment. A deciding factor in the success of the program is the dedication of the school library media specialist. For a school library media program to be successful it must possess the following characteristics:

- It must be **student-centered**. Students have the opportunity to learn to be efficient managers of information. They participate in learning activities that foster creativity and build critical thinking skills. Students collaborate with the school library media specialists to facilitate their learning experiences.
- The program works to **expand students' interests** and to foster a love of reading, listening and viewing.
- Works to **provide access to information** and assist students in evaluating that information so that it can be used effectively.

- The program **assists students in becoming lifelong learners** by teaching them to appreciate diverse perspectives, act responsibly with regard to information, build critical thinking skills, analyze information, and create products based upon the information acquired.
- The school library media specialist **collaborates with students and staff** to provide authentic learning experiences that integrate information skills into the curriculum. Collaboration is one of the most crucial components to the success of a school library media program.
- The school library media specialist **works as a leader** within the school to bring resources into the school as well as train others to use those resources.
- The school library media specialist **creates partnerships** within the community to further enhance educational opportunities for students.
- The school library media specialist provides **physical access to resources** that meet the needs of all populations.

Skill 1.5   Formulating a mission statement for the library media program that reflects overall school and district goals and objectives

The mission of any organization, business, or educational institution should evolve from the needs and expectations of its clientele. The mission of the school library media center must parallel the school's mission and attend to the users' needs for resources and services.

The school library media program should examine school and student characteristics.

School characteristics:

1. The mission of the school library media center should reflect and be in harmony with the school's stated mission.
2. The program's mission should reflect the curricular direction of the school: academic, vocational, or compensatory.
3. The mission should reflect the willingness of the administration and faculty to support the program.

Student characteristics:

1. The mission is influenced by pupil demographics: age, achievement and ability levels, reading levels, and learning styles.
2. The mission may indicate the students' interest in self-directed learning and exploratory reading.
3. The mission reflects support from parents and community groups.

Skill 1.6 **Recognizing the role of the library media program in providing equitable physical and intellectual access to information, ideas, and learning and teaching tools**

Each school has a unique population of students. The school library media coordinator must collaborate with both regular and special-education teachers to find resources that fill a wide array of student needs. Physical conditions need to be addressed. Accommodation of students in wheelchairs requires appropriate arrangement of furniture, width of aisles, and shelf heights. and aisle wide enough for wheelchair access. Visually impaired students may need special lighting or magnifying devices.

To promote equal access to services, the school library media coordinator should plan activities that allow all students to participate successfully. Post rules and signs in large print using pictures and the Braille alphabet. These reminders and cues provide assistance for easily distracted students. Special-education teachers may be able to provide additional insight when planning services, physical layout and collections.

Student abilities will influence collection decisions as well. Visually-impaired students may need books in Braille or large-print, auditory books, or software that reads web pages and scanned text.

The use of technology can enhance student access to resources. Some examples include:

- Special computing devices for students with mobility issues make technology accessible to them. These devices can be activated by moving a single muscle, blinking or other function.
- Built-in accommodations in software programs, such as Microsoft Word.
- Specialized software that translates typed text into Braille, sign language, or a different language.
- Digital technology to synthesize audio and work with digital images and video.
- Virtual field trips on the Internet.

COMPETENCY 0002 UNDERSTAND THE ROLES AND RESPONSIBILITIES OF THE LIBRARY MEDIA SPECIALIST

Skill 2.1 Applying strategies for creating a positive teaching and learning climate in the library media center

Because of the diversity of services provided in a modern school library media center, it is important to foster a user-friendly atmosphere, one in which the patron is not only welcomed as a user of resources but is also involved as a producer of ideas and materials.

The library media program, in considering the academic and personal needs of the user, should provide an atmosphere in which users can attain both basic skills and enrichment goals.

Factors that influence the atmosphere include:

1. Proximity to academic classes.
2. Aesthetic appearance.
3. Acoustical ceilings and floor coverings.
4. Adequate temperature control.
5. Adequate, non-glare lighting with controls for different types of viewing activities.
6. Comfortable, appropriately sized, and durable furnishings.
7. Diverse, plentiful, and current resources that are attractive to handle as well as easy to use.
8. Courteous, helpful personnel, using supervisory techniques that encourage self-exploration and creativity while protecting the rules of library etiquette.

Skill 2.2 Applying strategies for encouraging students to take responsibility for their own learning

Students need to know the variety of information resources and agencies available to them and be given frequent opportunities to use them in order to establish habit. By learning about the resources available outside the school, they will more likely pursue using these services in adulthood.

1. Inform them of **information resource-sharing networks**: public and academic libraries, Internet services, and community agencies. Schools in districts with fully automated public-library systems may provide online access to the public library catalog from a terminal at the school site. Public libraries may also offer online cataloging services that can be accessed from home computers and provide access to the Internet.
2. **Invite representatives from other information agencies** to promote their programs through the schools. Post public library hours, advertisements of lectures, book reviews, or other library activities; arrange for guest speakers from Internet providers or radio and television stations; and participate in field trips to other information centers

Skill 2.3 Demonstrating knowledge of the management functions of library media specialists with regard to services, facilities, personnel, and funding

One of the main goals of a school library media specialist is to determine the overall vision and mission of the media center. The vision of what the media center should be the focus of all other functions.

Once a direction has been established, the school library media specialist can use the **Library Learning Walk** to determine the strengths and weaknesses of the resources and overall program and begin to develop a course of improvement.

Policies and procedures must be developed to govern the overall operation of the media program. Using the mission as a guide, policies and procedures can be created or revised to meet changing needs.

The vision, mission, and all gathered data help to **identify specific funding** needs.

In preparation for **constructing the budget** for the school library media center, the school media professionals need to consider:

1. The **standards** set by the New York State Department of Education, local school boards, and regional accreditation associations. Changes in standards sometimes necessitate changes in local budget planning.
2. The **sources of funding** for the media center program (4.3.2).
3. The prioritized list of **program goals** and the cost of meeting them.

Determining the relationship between program goals and funding involve the study of:

1. **Past inventories** and projections of future needs.
2. Quantitative and qualitative **collection standards** at all levels.
3. School and district **curriculum plans**.
4. **Community needs**.
5. **Fiscal deadlines**.

TEACHER CERTIFICATION STUDY GUIDE

Skill 2.4 **Recognizing the importance of building and maintaining collaborative partnerships to support the library media program**

The school library media specialist must establish rapport with all groups in the school community. To promote this collaboration, representatives from these groups should be involved in the development, implementation, and evaluation of the school library media program.

1. Establish a library media **advisory committee.**
2. Solicit **expert advice of teachers** on selecting materials for the collection and weeding.
3. **Promote the program** and solicit suggestions for improvement.
4. Establish a reciprocal **working relationship with the school principal** and/or supervisor of media.
5. Conduct **workshops or lessons** on using the media center as a resource center.

Skill 2.5 **Recognizing the role of the library media specialist in providing expertise and advocacy in collection development and the use of information technology and resources**

It is the responsibility of the school library media specialist to provide resources that meet the needs for the population it serves. Therefore the school library media collection should include resources that are current, relevant to state and local curricula, and of interest to students and staff.

To ensure the collection matches the needs of the population, the school library media specialist must:

1. Conduct a **collection analysis.**
2. **Discard** any irrelevant or outdated materials.
3. Use professional **review publications** to keep abreast of new resources.
4. Provide staff and students the **opportunity to request materials**.
5. Develop a working **relationship with vendors** of books and media.

Access to resources requires an **automated catalog** that reflects the current status of the collection.

Technological resources play an important role in providing resources to staff and students. The school library media specialist must work to ensure all stakeholders have access to the technology available by:

1. **Maintaining** all equipment in proper working order.
2. Developing **policies and procedures** that govern the use of such resources.
3. **Promoting** the use of resources by staff, students, and parents.

COMPETENCY 0003 UNDERSTAND THE INSTRUCTIONAL PARTNER ROLE OF THE LIBRARY MEDIA SPECIALIST IN CURRICULUM DEVELOPMENT.

Skill 3.1 Demonstrating knowledge of basic principles of curriculum development and standardized practices

Curriculum is defined as the specific skills or objectives students should know or be able to perform when they complete a certain grade level. Curriculum development is a serious process. It takes place mostly at the state level, but local districts also develop curriculum for local purposes.

The process generally works through a **team approach**, utilizing classroom teachers known for their expertise in a particular subject. The team reviews current learning objectives to evaluate their validity and identify necessary changes.

Objectives are written as student **learning outcomes or goals**. A goal is a general statement, which is broken down into the skills needed to meet the goal. Specific examples regarding the mastery of the skill may be provided.

Every goal and skill that is listed must be **measurable**. The curriculum development process may also include the designing of appropriate assessments to measure a student's level of performance with a particular skill.

Evaluation of the curriculum is the most crucial step in the process. Through evaluation the new content is measured for effectiveness. After careful evaluation the goal or skill may once again be revised to promote the lifelong learning process for students.

The key factor in curriculum development is that is an **ongoing process**. Goals and skills must be continuously evaluated for effectiveness and restructured to ensure student success.

Skill 3.2 Demonstrating knowledge of integrating New York State Learning Standards and national information literacy standards into the school curriculum

National information literacy standards stress that information literate students:

- Can access, evaluate and use information effectively.
- Pursue, appreciate and strive for excellence when seeking information.
- Understand the necessity of a democratic society.
- Strive to be responsible citizens.
- work to generate more information

There are direct correlations between the national standards and the New York State Learning standards.

- Access to information: English Language Arts Standards 1 and 2; Math, Science, and Technology Standard 2; Social Studies Standards 1-5
- Evaluates information: English Language Arts Standard 3; Math, Science, and Technology Standard 6
- Use of information: English Language Arts Standard 4; Math, Science, and Technology Standards 2, 5, and 7
- Pursues knowledge and information: Career Development and Occupational Studies Standard 1
- Appreciates information: Arts Standard 2
- Strives for excellence in searching for information: Career Development and Occupational Studies Standards 3a and 3b
- Necessity of a democratic society: Social Studies Standard 5
- Being a responsible citizen: Socials Studies Standard 5
- Generates information: Social Studies Standard 5

Skill 3.3 Identifying types and characteristics of various instructional materials and resources (e.g., overhead transparencies, multimedia presentations)

Technology has changed the instructional resources now available to schools. A wide array of resources can be found, in multiple formats. Types of resources that are used in schools can include:

- **Overhead transparencies** are still a viable tool for instruction. Transparencies are easily created using computer software and films meant for either inkjet or laser printers.
- **Multimedia Presentations** are used to accentuate material presented to students. The format is often more appealing than transparencies, but availability of equipment can be an issue.
- **Audio recordings:** Older formats such as vinyl records have been replaced by cassette tapes then CDs. Podcasts or computerized records are currently a popular format. These recordings can be played directly from the computer or downloaded onto various devices.
- **Video recordings:** Filmstrips have given way to video, which adds animation. It is found in such formats as videotape, DVD, Blue Ray disc, and video streamed from online sources.
- **Print material:** Libraries are still stocked with circulating books. Books are also found in audio format as well as electronic ebooks.
- **Computer Software** supports many learning opportunities. It can be loaded either on a single machine or on a server, which allows shared access throughout the school's network. Network access requires special licenses.

- **Online Programs:** Many resources once housed within the walls of the media center can now be accessed online. Some resources are subscription-based but are still considerably cheaper than upgrading software on CD-ROMs. One disadvantage of this format can be the space it takes up on the district's bandwidth. Online resources containing a great deal of video can cause a network to perform far more slowly.

Skill 3.4   Examining considerations related to the design and production of instructional materials (e.g. intended audience) and applying procedures for producing and reproducing various types of instructional materials

In the last twenty years, audiovisual materials, once considered supplementary to instruction, have become instructional media, integral parts of the instructional process. Students and teachers should learn not only to use commercial products but to design and produce their own materials. It is appropriate for faculty to produce their own resources when:

1. Commercial products are unavailable, unsuited to learning styles/preferences/environments, or too costly.
2. Teaching styles indicate a preference for noncommercial products.
3. Teachers have the expertise and necessary equipment for original production.

It is appropriate for students to produce their own resources when:

1. Achieving understanding with nonverbal means of expression.
2. Communicating ideas and information to others.
3. Expressing creativity.
4. Demonstrating mastery of lesson objectives by alternative means.

Having determined that it is appropriate to use teacher- or student-produced media, it is necessary to determine which media should be produced to meet the specific instructional need. School library media specialists may produce media for two purposes:

1. To make presentations for information skills instruction, other teacher-directed activities, or testing.
2. To make materials to be placed directly in the hands of students.

Many excellent books on media instruction detail the instructional uses of media formats. A few will be summarized here.

1. **Introduction.** Formats that allow large-group listening or viewing are appropriate for introducing new materials: filmstrips, films, slide-tapes, computer projections, overhead transparencies, and videotapes. With young learners, display boards with large print and audiocassettes for storytelling with nonreaders are most effective.
2. **Application.** During this phase, media that lend themselves to individual or small group use are needed. As students investigate the subject matter, organize that information, practice, or demonstrate understanding, they may create any of several types of media. With young children these would include manipulatives: building blocks, letters, numbers, or shapes in cloth, plastic, or wood. Older students create photographs, slides, audiocassette tapes, or videotapes. Some secondary students might even design their own computer programs. Students at all levels can be taught to use computer design software to create multimedia productions.

The application of media production techniques helps the producers, adult or child, to clarify their own objectives and determine the exact format to best present their ideas and achieve their goals. A lesson on distinguishing the calls of local birds might use sound recording, while a lesson on recognizing plumage uses slides or videotape. Students preparing a study of estuarine ecology can incorporate video and computer graphics derived from electron-microscope imagery to demonstrate types of microorganisms in the local river.

Skill 3.5 **Demonstrating knowledge of methods for sharing information with faculty and staff for professional enrichment**

Designing a staff development activity follows a basic lesson profile with special considerations for adult learners.

1. **Analysis of learning styles.** Adult learners are more receptive to role playing and individual performance before a group. Learner motivation is more internal, but some external motivations, such as release time, compensatory time, in service credit or some written recognition, might be discussed with the principal.
2. **Assessment of learner needs.** Conduct a survey among teachers to determine which media or equipment they want to learn more about. Consider such environmental factors as time, place, and temperature. Since many in-service activities occur after school, taking the lesson to the teachers in their own classrooms may make them more comfortable, especially if they can have a reviving afternoon snack. If they must come to the media center, serve refreshments.
3. **Select performance objectives.** Determine exactly what the teacher should be able to do at the end of a successful in service session.
4. **Plan activities to achieve objectives.** Demonstrate the skill to be taught, involve the participants in active performance or production, and allow for practice and feedback.
5. **Select appropriate resources.** Ensure that all materials and equipment are ready and in good functioning order on the day of the in-service training.
6. **Select the instructor.** Either the school library media specialist or a faculty member should conduct these onsite in-service sessions, unless the complexity or novelty of the technology requires an outside expert.
7. **Provide continuing support.** The instructor or designated substitute should be available after the training for reinforcement.
8. **Evaluation.** Determine the effectiveness of the session and consider modifications in future training based on the recommendations.

TEACHER CERTIFICATION STUDY GUIDE

COMPETENCY 0004 UNDERSTAND PROFESSIONAL STANDARDS, LEGAL REQUIREMENTS, AND ETHICAL ISSUES IN THE LIBRARY MEDIA PROGRAM.

Skill 4.1 Identifying professional responsibilities of the library media specialist (e.g. ensuring equitable access to information, instructing and training other members of the learning community about library media resources and their uses, serving as an advocate for students and the library media program, recognizing and addressing issues of bias and diversity)

The following summarizes AASL/AECT guidelines.

The role of the school library media specialist is threefold.

The information specialist meets program needs by providing:

1. Access to the facility and materials that is non-restrictive, economically, ethnically, or physically.
2. Communication to teachers, students, administrators, and parents concerning new materials, services, or technologies.
3. Efficient retrieval and information sharing systems.

The teacher specialist is responsible for:

1. Integrating information skills into the content curriculum.
2. Providing access to and instruction in the use of technology.
3. Planning jointly with classroom teachers the use and production of media appropriate to learner needs.
4. Using various instructional methods to provide staff development in policies, procedures, media production, and technology use.

The instructional consultant uses expertise to:

1. Participate in curriculum development and assessment.
2. Assist teachers in acquiring information skills that they can incorporate into classroom instruction.
3. Design a scope and sequence of teaching information skills.
4. Provide leadership in the use and assessment of information technologies.

Skill 4.2 Demonstrating knowledge of ethical responsibilities of library media personnel on various situations

All libraries have certain guidelines that should be followed. The American Library Association has created a Library Bill of Rights while the Association of Educational Communications and Technology has designed a Code of Ethics.

LIBRARY & MEDIA SPECIALIST

The Library Bill of Rights agrees that libraries are places to obtain information and develop ideas. A brief description of each policy is as follows:

- Resources should not be excluded because of the author's origin, background, or views.
- Resources should include a representation of all points of view.
- Censorship of information should be challenged.
- A person should not be denied access to a library because of origin, age, background, or views.
- Libraries that make space available to the public should do so on an equitable basis.

AECT's Code of Ethics includes a preamble and three sections.

The Preamble briefly describes the code of ethics.

Section 1, Commitment to the Individual, explains that a library should encourage independent learning, protect individual rights, promote professional development with regards to technology, should provide and educational program that develops the learner, and follow the first amendment.

Section 2, Commitment to Society, states that members shall honestly represent their organizations, should not accept gifts of favors that would impair their professional judgment, and shall follow fair and equitable practices.

Section 3, Commitment to the Profession, states that members should treat all other members fairly, should not exploit their membership for monetary gain, shall abide by and educate others in copyright law, and shall observe all laws that relate to their profession.

Skill 4.3   Applying professional and legal standards and guidelines in various library media contexts

Intellectual Freedom: Ethical principles

The principles of intellectual freedom are guaranteed by the First Amendment to the Constitution of the United States. They are reinforced in the Library Bill of Rights adapted by the ALA in 1948, the AECT's statement on intellectual freedom (1978), the freedom to read and review statements of the ALA (1953 and 1979), and the Students Right to Read statement of the National Council of English Teachers.

The principles as they relate to children are:

1. Freedom of access to information in all formats through activities that develop critical thinking and problem solving skills.
2. Freedom of access to ideas that present a variety of points of view through activities that teach discriminating reading.
3. Freedom to acquire information reflective of the intellectual, physical, and social growth of the user.

The school library media specialist is responsible for developing and maintaining a collection development policy that ensures these freedoms. For methods of handling complaints, see Skill 8.3.

Intellectual Freedom: Legal Principles

Court rulings have ambiguously addressed the issue of censorship. In 1972, the U.S. Court of Appeals for the Second Circuit (*President's Council* v. *Community School Board No. 25, New York City*) ruled in favor of the removal of a library book, finding no constitutional issue in the addition or withdrawal of books in a public school library.

In 1976, the Court of Appeals for the Sixth Circuit (*Minarcini* v. *Strongsville City School District*) ruled against the removal of Joseph Heller's *Catch 22* and two Kurt Vonnegut novels on the grounds that removal of books from a school library is a burden on the freedom of classroom discussion and an infringement of the First Amendment's guarantee of an individual's "right to know."

A Massachusetts district court (*Right to Read Defense Committee* v. *School Board of the City of Chelsea*) ordered the school board to return to the high school library a poetry anthology that contained "objectionable and filthy" language. The court asserted that the school had control over curriculum but not library collections, which allow the student to expand on ideas taught in the classroom.

Three cases in the 1980s dealt with challenging the removal of materials from high school libraries. The case of *Zykan* v. *Warsaw Community School Corporation, Indiana*, recognized a broad but not unlimited authority of school boards to remove books from school libraries. The case of *Board of Education, Island Trees Union Free School District 26 (New York)* v. *Pico* reached the Supreme Court in 1982 after the U.S. Court of Appeals for then Second Circuit had reversed a lower court ruling granting the school board the right to remove nine books which had been deemed "anti-American, anti-Semitic, anti-Christian and just plain filthy." The Supreme Court in a 5-4 ruling upheld the Court of Appeals' ruling and the nine books were returned. Justice Blackmun's concurring opinion, however, continued to foster ambiguity by claiming that an infringement of the First Amendment existed only if the intent was to deny free access to ideas. Ultimately, the issue hinged on a school board's authority in determining the selection of optional rather than required reading. Library books, being optional, should not be denied to users.

Confidentiality

Suggested procedures include the following:

1. When a request is made for confidential information, explain the confidentiality policy.
2. Consult with the appropriate legal adviser to determine if such process, order, or subpoena is in good form and if there is a just cause for its issuance.
3. If the process is not in proper form, or if just cause has not been shown, the library should insist that this be remedied before any records are released.
4. Generally a subpoena *duces tecum* (bring your records) requires the responsible library officer to attend court or to testify. It also may require that certain circulation records be submitted.
5. Staff should be trained and required to report any threats not supported by a process, order, or subpoena concerning the records.
6. If any problems arise refer them to the responsible legal counsel.

Skill 4.4 **Demonstrating knowledge of issues related to copyright and intellectual property and of legislation affecting library media programs**

The federal courts have ruled on copyright issues. The 1975 ruling in the case of *Williams & Wilkins Co.* v. *U.S.* provided guidance to legislators in preparing the fair-use provisions of the 1976 Copyright Act.

It ruled that entire articles may be mass-duplicated for uses that advance the public welfare without doing economic harm to the publishers. This ruling provides encouragement to educators that fair use may be interpreted more liberally.

In 1984, the ruling in the *Sony Corp. of America* v. *Universal City Studios, Inc.* placed the burden of proving infringement on the plaintiff. The Supreme Court upheld the right of individuals to videotape television programs off-air for noncommercial use. Thus, a copyright holder must prove that the use of videotaped programming is intentionally harmful. Civil suits against educators require the plaintiff to prove that the existing or potential market would be negatively affected by use of these programs in a classroom setting.

Under the 1976 Copyright Act, educators have the benefit of greater leeway in copying than any other group. Many printed instructional materials carry statements that allow production of multiple copies for classroom use, provided they adhere to the "Guidelines for Classroom Copying in Nonprofit Educational Institutions." Teachers may duplicate enough copies to provide one per student per course provided that they meet the tests of brevity, spontaneity, and cumulative effect.

1. **Brevity test:**
    a. Poetry: suggested maximum 250 words.
    b. Prose: one complete essay, story, or article less than 2500 words or excerpts of no more than 1000 words or 10% of the work, whichever is shortest. (Children's books with text under 2500 words may not be copied in their entirety. No more than two pages containing 10% of the text may be copied.)
    c. Illustrations: charts, drawings, cartoons, etc. are limited to one per book or periodical article.
2. **Spontaneity test:** Copying that does not fall under the brevity test normally requires the publisher's permission for duplication. Allowances are made, however, if "the inspiration and decision to use the work" occur too soon prior to classroom use for permission to be sought in writing.
3. **Cumulative effect test:** Even in the case of short poems or prose, it is preferable to make only one copy. Three short items from one work, however, are allowed during one class term. Reuse of copied material from term to term is expressly forbidden. Compilation of works into anthologies to be used in place of purchasing texts is prohibited.

The 1976 Copyright Act, especially section 107 dealing with fair use, created legislative criteria to follow based on judicial precedents. In 1978, when the law took effect, it set regulations for the duration and scope of copyright, specified authors' rights, and set monetary penalties for infringement.

The statutory penalty may be waived by the court for an employee of a nonprofit educational institution where the employee can prove fair-use intent.

Fair use, especially important to educators, is meant to create a balance between copyright protection and the needs of learners for access to protected material. Fair use is judged by the purpose of the use, the nature of the work (whether creative or informational), the quantity of the work for use, and the market effect.

In essence, if a *portion* of a work is used to benefit the learner with no intent to deprive the author of his profits, fair use is granted. Recently, fair use has been challenged most in cases of videotaping off-air of television programs. Guidelines too numerous to delineate here affect copying audiovisual materials and computer software. Most distributors place written regulations in the packaging of these products. Allowances for single backup copies in the event of damage to the original are granted.

Section 108 is pertinent to libraries in that it permits reproducing a single copy of an entire work if no financial gain is derived, if the library is public or archival, and if the copyright notice appears on all copies.

In any event in which violation of the law is a concern, the safest course of action is to seek written permission from the publisher of the copyrighted work. If permission is granted, a copy of that permission should accompany any duplicates.

A school library media specialist who becomes aware of suspected infringement of copyright should follow certain procedures:

1. Determine if a violation has actually occurred. Never accuse or report alleged instances to a higher authority without verification.
2. If an instance is verified, tactfully inform the violator of the specific criteria to use so that future violations can be avoided. Presented properly, the information will probably be accepted as constructive.
3. If the advice is unheeded and further infractions occur, bring them to the attention of the teacher's supervisor (team leader or department chair), who can handle the matter as an evaluation procedure.
4. Inform the person who has reported the alleged violation of the procedures being used.

SUBAREA II. LIBRARY MEDIA RESOURCES

COMPETENCY 0005 UNDERSTAND THE RELATIONSHIP BETWEEN THE LIBRARY MEDIA PROGRAM AND INFORMATION RESOURCES AND SERVICES BEYOND THE SCHOOL.

Skill 5.1 Demonstrating understanding of the role of libraries in a democratic society to sustain lifelong learning

Libraries are charged with providing equitable access to resources containing a variety of viewpoints and cultural perspectives. This access to information is one of the fundamental rights of a citizen within a democratic society.

With access to information comes responsibility. School library media specialists play the role of mediators in helping students to appreciate rights of others to express their own points of view.

When putting this into practice the school library media specialist can guide a student to a deeper understanding of this principle by:

- Organizing cultural awareness days where students explore various cultures.
- Involving students in dilemmas pertaining to accessing information.
- Leading a study on the influences of various cultures within their own community.

Skill 5.2 Recognizing the role of the library media program in connecting teachers and students to local, district, state, national, and global resources

Students need to know the diverse information resources and agencies available to them and be given frequent opportunities to use them in order to establish habit. By learning about the resources available outside the school, they will more likely pursue using these services in adulthood.

1. Inform them of resource sharing networks, such as public libraries, Internet services, and community agencies. Some schools in districts with fully automated public library systems may provide online access to the public library catalog from a terminal at the school site. Public libraries also offer online catalogs that can be accessed from home computers and some are now providing access to the Internet. Academic libraries often encourage high school students to use their resources.

2. Invite representatives from other information agencies to promote their programs through the schools. Post public library hours, advertisements of lectures, book reviews, or other library activities; arrange for guest speakers from Internet providers or radio and television stations; and participate in field trips to other information centers

Skill 5.3   Demonstrating knowledge of the characteristics and uses of information resources and services beyond the school (e.g. electronic services, public libraries, interlibrary loan, state service providers for special populations)

Resource sharing has always been an integral part of education. Before the technology revolution, the sharing was done within schools or departments and between teachers. Now it is possible to access information around the world.

Resource sharing is a way of:

1. Providing a broader information base to enable users to find and access the resources that provide the needed information.
2. Reducing or containing media center costs.
3. Establishing cooperation with other resource providers that encourage mutual planning and standardization of control.

Resource sharing systems include:

4. **Interlibrary loan.** The advent of computer databases has simplified the process of locating sources in other libraries.
    d. Local public library collections can be accessed from terminals in the media center. Physical access depends on going to the branch where the material is housed.
    e. Many colleges and universities libraries loan materials to school libraries through mail or delivery networks
5. **Networking systems**.
    a. Email, typed chats, video chats, and online calling are tools for communication in real time.
    b. Online services offer access to a specific menu of locations. Monthly fees and/or time charges must be budgeted.
    c. NOVELNY (New York Online Virtual Electronic Library) provides 24/7 access to a wide array of resources including: books, magazines, newspapers, and reference materials to all New Yorkers free of charge.
    d. Academic libraries often allow outside users to access research databases onsite.
    e. Individual city or county network systems. These are community-sponsored networks, often part of the public library system, which provides Internet access for the price of a local phone call. Search time is usually limited in order to allow more users access.

      f.   Online continuing education programs offer courses/ degrees through home study. Large school districts provide lessons for homebound students or home school advocates.

      g.   Bulletin boards allow individuals or groups to converse electronically with persons in another place.

6. **Telecommunications.** Distance learning uses television, telephone, and the Internet. Universities or networks of universities provide workshops, conferences, and college credit courses for educators as well as courses for senior high school students in subjects that could not generate adequate class counts in their home schools. Large school districts offer broadcast programming for homebound/home school students. Students can interact with instructors by telephone or the Internet.

COMPETENCY 0006 UNDERSTAND TYPES AND CHARACTERISTICS OF PRINT, NONPRINT, AND ELECTRONIC RESOURCES

Skill 6.1 Demonstrating knowledge of types, characteristics and uses of print resources

Reference materials are generally housed in a special location within the media center. They are there for patrons to use, but generally do not circulate outside the library. Examples of reference materials are almanacs, dictionaries, encyclopedias, bibliographies, indexes, atlases, and manuals.

Circulating materials can be borrowed for use outside the library.

NOVELNY allows New York residents online access to many types of print resources.

Skill 6.2 Demonstrating knowledge of types, characteristics and uses of nonprint resources, demonstrating knowledge of types, characteristics, and uses of electronic resources

With the flood of technological advances in the past few decades, school library media centers have a wealth of non-print information available.

Examples include:

- **Computerized databases** include online dictionaries, encyclopedias, and periodical indexes. These databases are easily searched using keywords and generally contain cross-references to similar information. The speed of computerized databases dramatically reduces search time.
- **Online catalogs** of the school library media center's resources and other collections. They can generally be searched by keyword, author, or subject heading.
- **CD-ROM and DVD.** Information in these formats include electronic atlases, encyclopedias, and simulations among other topics. The high storage capacity allows the addition of relevant audio and video to the text found in the print version.
- **Video** is found in a wide variety of formats. DVD is the preferred medium because of its density of storage and greater durability. Videotapes in various formats are still part of the resources found in many school library media centers, since school budgets may be inadequate for conversion to DVD. Many video cameras used in schools utilize other media for recording. As technology changes and the format for videos improve, schools will eventually move to newer formats as they arise.

Online videos are often cost-effective supplements to the collection. A variety of educational videos can be found online. Companies such as United Streaming focus on providing quality educational videos. The main issue with viewing videos online is the bandwidth these resources require. Bandwidth is the amount of information that can be sent over a network. When a file such as a video takes up a large part of the bandwidth other resources begin to slow down. Careful consideration and consultation with the network administrator is necessary before viewing videos online.

- **Audio,** including spoken books and is also found in a variety of formats. CD is the preferred format because of its greater density of storage and durability. Audio is also found in the format of cassette tapes. As cassettes become worn or damaged they are being replaced by CDs. Audio clips can be found online. Podcasts are audio files found online, many of which are in the format of a radio broadcast. The use of streaming audio from the Internet uses up a network's bandwidth, but to a lesser extent than video. The issue for using the older format of vinyl records, is the cost of acquiring and maintaining equipment.

Skill 6.3   Recognizing and comparing advantages and limitations of various resources and formats

In comparing various types of information formats, each has their strengths and weaknesses.

- **Print resources** are very important for young learners. They need to touch and feel and learn how to use a book. Books, however, can be more cumbersome and require more time to find information.
- **Computerized resources** are easier means of searching for information. Their interactivity provides more in-depth understanding than what is gained from print alone. One disadvantage is that some students find it difficult to read large articles on the computer and will often opt to print the articles.
- **Video** is necessary to the success of visual learners. Schools must have the equipment to play each type of video used. The use of online video in conjunction with other network applications needs to be closely monitored to keep the network from becoming severely hampered.
- **Audio** is a very effective tool for auditory learners, but less interactive than some other formats. It requires special equipment and can consume network bandwidth.

TEACHER CERTIFICATION STUDY GUIDE

COMPETENCY 0007 UNDERSTAND TYPES AND CHARACTERISTICS OF LITERATURE FOR CHILDREN AND YOUNG ADULTS

Skill 7.1 Demonstrating knowledge of various forms and genres of literature (e.g. biography, poetry, drama, science fiction)

Popular genres and authors in children's literature include:

- **Juvenile fiction** consists of stories based upon imagination, rather than fact. Popular writers for this genre include Judy Blume, Robert Cormier, Rosa Guy, Virginia Hamilton, S. E. Hinton, M. E. Kerr, Harry Mazer, Norma Fox Mazer, Richard Newton Peck, Cynthia Voight, and Paul Zindel.
- **Fantasy:** works that focus on the supernatural or incorporate magic. Famous fantasy writer for young adults include: Piers Anthony, Ursula LeGuin, and Ann McCaffrey
- **Horror** includes scary or horrific stories on such themes as monsters, paranormal events, and the spirit world. Popular horror writers include: V.C. Andrews, and Stephen King
- **Science fiction** consists of stories based on technology or science, often in a future setting. They may include beings from another planet and time travel. Popular authors include: Isaac Asimov, Ray Bradbury, Arthur Clarke, Frank Herbert, Larry Niven, and H. G. Wells.
- **Folk tales** are stories that have been passed down through generations by word of mouth.
- **Historical fiction** is centered on real or fictional characters in the context of a historical event.
- **Picture books** and picture story books are most often works of fiction that are colorfully illustrated. Notable illustrators of children's books include Marcia Brown, Leo and Diane Dillon, Nonny Hogrogian, David Macaulay, Emily Arnold McCully, Allen Say, Maurice Sendak, Chris Van Allsburg, and David Wiesner.

Skill 7.2 Identifying characteristics of literature for children and young adults

Children's/adolescent literature of the last 50 years has grown to thousands of new titles per year. Many tend to the trendy, since the authors and publishers are very aware of the market and the social changes affecting their products. Books are selected for libraries because of their social, psychological, and intellectual value. Collections must also contain materials that recognize cultural and ethnic needs. Because so many popular titles, especially for young adults, deal with controversial subjects, school library media specialists are faced with juggling the preferences of their student patrons with the need to provide worthwhile literature and maintain intellectual freedom in the face of increasing censorship. Books such as Robert Cormier's *Chocolate War*, *Beyond the Chocolate War,* and *Fade* deal with the darker side of teen life. Paul Zindel's *Pigman* and *The Undertaker's Gone Bananas* deal with the stresses in teen life with a touch of humor.

Books for young children teach about their relationships to the world around them and to other people and things in that world. They help him learn how things operate and how to overcome their fears. Like the still popular fairy tales of previous centuries, some of today's popular children's books are fantasies or allegories, such as Robert O'Brien's *Mrs. Frisby and the Rats of NIMH*.

Popular books for preadolescents often deal with establishing relationships with members of the opposite sex (*Sweet Valley High* series) and learning to cope with their changing bodies, personalities, or life situations as in Judy Blume's *Are You There, God? It's Me, Margaret*. Adolescents are still interested in the fantasy and science fiction genres as well as popular juvenile fiction. Middle school students still read Laura Ingalls Wilder's *Little House on the Prairie* series and the mysteries of the Hardy boys and Nancy Drew. Teens may value the works of Emily and Charlotte Brontë, Willa Cather, Jack London, William Shakespeare, and Mark Twain as much as those of Piers Anthony, S.E. Hinton, Madeleine L'Engle, Stephen King, and J.R.R. Tolkien because they're fun to read whatever their underlying worth may be.

Skill 7.3 Recognizing developmental factors that should be considered when selecting literature for individual students

Helping students find literature that meets their needs developmentally is essential to improving their learning.

Preschool- through kindergarten-age students need literature that they will find enjoyable and that helps them to learn language patterns. The story needs to be easy for these young readers to follow. Books to be read independently should have plenty of picture support. Books to be read to students need to be engaging and provide opportunities for students to interact with the text.

Students in **first and second grades** are developing literacy skills. They begin constructing meaning and building their sight-word vocabulary. As independent readers these students need books that utilize various cuing systems, such as syntax, semantics and the use of picture support. These students are beginning to see themselves as readers.

Third and fourth graders should have acquired basic reading skills and are working to build fluency. They are beginning to read books with fewer pictures and longer stories. They are also beginning to use textbooks as a information sources and must begin to read for deeper meaning as well as for enjoyment.

Beyond the elementary grades, students read for a variety of reasons. They are most likely fluent readers. When reading for pleasure it is important for students to select books that are of interest. They students are also expected to read for information in textbooks and other information resources.

Skill 7.4 Applying strategies and activities that promote the appreciation and enjoyment of reading

One of the best ways for a school library media program to promote appreciation and enjoyment of reading is to provide a quality, well-balanced collection of books and other resources that address various learning styles. This collection should be based upon state requirements, curricular requirements and student interests. Types of resources could include print materials, audio books, books on video and electronic books.

The media specialist plays a crucial role in promoting literature appreciation through the organization of literature appreciation activities. These activities could include book clubs, creating a reader's theater, puppet shows, etc.

Developing family activities that occur before, during, or after school hours can help promote a love or reading. Popular events include author visits and family reading nights.

Another fairly simple way to promote a love of reading is to arrange the media center in such a way that resources are easy to find and that space is provided for individual, small group and large group reading activities.

COMPETENCY 0008 UNDERSTAND ISSUES AND PROCEDURES RELATED TO COLLECTION DEVELOPMENT

Skill 8.1 Identifying sources for the acquisition of materials and equipment for the library media program

When selecting resources for a school library, it is important to collaborate with teachers and follow district and state selection policies. Finding the resources can be a daunting task because there are many sources of information.

The best places to begin are review publications such as:

- *School Library Journal*
- *Booklist*
- *The Horn Book*
- *Book Review Digest*

Each of these provides concise reviews on current books. *Book Review Digest* is a collective guide that provides excerpts from the other sources listed.

Other places to locate resources include:

1. **Collection lists** designed for elementary, middle, or secondary schools or for special content schools, such as vocational or performing arts. These lists are used most often for opening a new school library media center. School library media specialists and review committees customize these lists to user needs.
2. **Publisher's catalogs** are good starting points for locating specific titles and comparison shopping.
3. **Vendors** representing one or more publishers. It is important to establish good relationships with vendors, who have access to demonstration materials and can make them available for review. Naturally, they want to sell their employers' products; most, however, are familiar with their competitors' product lines and work collaboratively to help schools secure the most appropriate materials.
4. **Bibliographic indexes** of subject specific titles with summaries. These indexes are not free and are most cost effective if housed in the district professional library. The same is true of *Books in Print*. Because its contents change significantly from year to year, many districts cannot justify its cost, relying instead on direct communication with publishers to determine a book's status.
5. *Publisher's Weekly* provides information on the latest releases, current topics, and book reviews.

Another way to provide a wide variety of literature is to include books that have been noted by organizations that specialize in reading. Each year the American Library Association, Children's Book Council and International Reading Association publish lists of notable books for children. Book awards are another source for lists of quality literature. Two of the most widely recognized awards are the Caldecott and Newberry Awards. Each year an outstanding illustrator of a children's book is honored for their outstanding work by being presented with the Caldecott Medal. This award was created in honor of Randolph Caldecott and is distributed annually by the Association for Library Service for Children. It was first presented in 1938.

Award winners for the past fifteen years include:

- 2008 *The Invention of Hugo Cabret* by Brian Selznick
- 2007 *Flotsam* by David Wiesner
- 2006 *The Hello, Goodbye Window* illustrated by Chris Raschka and written by Norton Juster
- 2005 *Kitten's First Full Moon* by Kevin Henkes
- 2004 *The Man Who Walked Between the Towers* by Mordicai Gerstein
- 2003 *My Friend Rabbit* by Eric Rohmann
- 2002 *The Three Pigs* by David Wiesner
- 2001 *So You Want to Be President?* Illustrated by David Small, written by Judith St. George
- 2000 *Had a Little Overcoat* Simms Taback
- 1999 **Snowflake Bentley**, Illustrated by Mary Azarian, text by Jacqueline Briggs Martin
- 1998 *Rapunzel* by Paul O. Zelinsky
- 1997 *Golem* by David Wisniewski
- 1996 *Officer Buckle and Gloria* by Peggy Rathmann
- 1995 *Smoky Night*, illustrated by David Diaz; text: Eve Bunting
- 1994 *Grandfather's Journey* by Allen Say; text: edited by Walter Lorraine
- 1993 *Mirette on the High Wire* by Emily Arnold McCully

Bookseller John Newbery was the first to publish literature for children on any scale in the second half of 18th century England, the great outpouring of children's literature came 100 years later in the Victorian Age. Novels such as Charles Dickens' *Oliver Twist*, Robert Louis Stevenson's *Treasure Island*, and Rudyard Kipling's *Jungle Book*, though not written for children alone, have become classics in children's literature. These books not only helped them understand the world they lived in but satisfied their sense of adventure.

The Newbery Award was created in honor of John Newbery in 1922. It is presented to an author of the most notable children's or young adult work of fiction.

Newbery award-winning books for the past fifteen years include:

- 2007 ***The Higher Power of Lucky*** written by Susan Patron, illustrated by Matt Phelan
- 2006- ***Criss Cross*** by Lynne Rae Perkins
- 2005 ***Kira-Kira*** by Cynthia Kadohata
- 2004 ***The Tale of Despereaux: Being the Story of a Mouse, a Princess, Some Soup, and a Spool of Thread*** by Kate DiCamillo, illustrated by Timothy Basil Ering
- 2003- ***Crispin: The Cross of Lead*** by Avi
- 2002 ***A Single Shard*** by Linda Sue Park
- 2001 ***A Year Down Yonder*** by by Richard Peck
- 2000 ***Bud, Not Buddy*** by Christopher Paul Curtis
- 1999 ***Holes*** by Louis Sachar
- 1998 ***Out of the Dust*** by Karen Hesse
- 1997 ***The View from Saturday*** by E.L. Konigsburg
- 1996 ***The Midwife's Apprentice*** by Karen Cushman
- 1995 ***Walk Two Moons*** by Sharon Creech
- 1994 ***The Giver*** by Lois Lowry

Two of the many other awards that have come about in recent years include:

The **Coretta Scott King Award** is presented to outstanding African Americans authors and illustrators for their outstanding educational contributions.

The **Laura Ingalls Wilder Award** honors an author or illustrator whose books have made a significant and lasting contribution to literature for children. The books must be published in the United States.

Skill 8.2 **Developing and applying criteria for evaluating and selecting resources and equipment that will enable the library media program to support the school's mission and objectives**

Each school library media center should develop a policy tailored to the philosophy and objectives of that school's educational program. This policy provides guidelines by which all participants in the selection process can get insight into their responsibilities. The policy statement should reflect the following factors.

1. Compatibility with district, state, regional, and national guidelines (1.2).
2. Adherence to the principles of intellectual freedom and the specifics of copyright law.
3. Recognition of the rights of individuals or groups to challenge policies, procedures, or selected items and the establishment of procedures for dealing fairly with such challenges.
4. Recognition of users' needs and interests, including community demographics.

The policy should include the school library media center's mission and the criteria used in the selection process. General criteria for the selection of all media include

1. **Authenticity.** Media should be accurate, current, and authoritative. Copyright or printing dates are indicators of currency, but examination of content is often necessary to determine the relevance of the subject matter to its intended use. Research into the reputations of contributors and comparison to other materials by the same producer will provide insight into its literary quality.
2. **Subject matter appropriateness** includes relevance to the school's educational objectives, scope of coverage, treatment and arrangement of content, importance of content to the user, and appropriateness to users' ability levels and learning styles.
3. **Appeal.** Consideration of the artistic quality and language appropriateness will help in the selection of media that students will enjoy using. Properly selected materials should stimulate creativity and inspire further learning.

Steps in writing a collection development plan include:

1. Knowledge of the existing collection or the ability to create a new collection.
2. Knowledge of the external environment (the school and community).
3. Assessment of school programs and user needs.
4. Development of overall policies and procedures.
5. Guidelines for specific selection decisions.
6. Criteria for evaluating titles for selection.
7. Establishment of a process for planning and implementing the collection plan.
8. Establishment of acquisition policies and procedures.
9. Establishment of maintenance program.
10. Establishment of procedures for evaluating the collection.

Procedures for implementing the plan include:

1. Learning the collection. A library media specialist, new to a school with an existing collection, should use several approaches to becoming familiar with the collection.
    a. Browse the shelves. Note your degree of familiarity with titles. Examine items that are unfamiliar to you. Determine the relationship between the materials on similar subjects in different formats. Include the reference and professional collections in your browsing. Consider the accessibility of various media and the ease with which they can be located by users.
    b. Locate the center's procedures manual. Determine explanations for any seeming irregularities in the collection.
    c. Determine if any portions of the collection are housed in areas outside the media center.

2. A library media specialist who is required to create a new collection should:
   a. Consult with the district director about new school collection policies.
   b. Examine the collections of other comparable schools.
   c. Investigate companies, such as Baker and Taylor, that establish new collections based on criteria provided by the school.
3. Learning about the community.
   a. Examine the relationship of the media center to the total school program and other information agencies.
   b. Become familiar with the school, cultural, economic and political characteristics of the community and their influence on the schools.
4. Studying the school's curriculum and the needs of the users (students and faculty).
   a. Determine the proportions of basic skills to enrichment offerings, academic or vocational courses, and requirements and electives.
   b. Determine the ability levels and grouping techniques for learners.
   c. Determine instructional objectives of teachers in various content areas or grade levels (3.13).
5. Examining existing policies and procedures for correlation to data acquired in researching the school and community.
6. Examining specific selection procedures to determine if guidelines are best met.
7. Examining evaluation criteria for effectiveness in maintaining an appropriate collection.
8. Examine the process to determine that accurate procedures are in place to meet the criteria.
9. Examine the acquisition plan. Determine the procedure by which materials are ordered, received, paid for and processed.
10. Examine maintenance procedures for repairing or replacing materials and equipment, replacing consumables, and discarding non-repairable items.
11. Examine the collection to determine if policies and procedures are contributing to quality and quantity.

Procedures for maintaining the collection are perhaps the most important in the collection plan. The plan itself must provide efficient, economical procedures for keeping materials and equipment in usable condition.

Maintenance policies for equipment and some policies for materials are determined at the district level (4.6.3). Procedures to satisfy these policies are followed at the building level.

1. Replacement or discard of damaged items based on comparison of repair and replacement costs. Districts usually maintain repair contracts with external contractors for major repairs that cannot be done at the school or district media service center.
2. Equipment inventory and records on repair or disposal. Usage records help with the transfer of usable items from school to school.
3. Book bindery contracts.

Policies and procedures for periodic inspection, preventive maintenance and cleaning, and minor repairs are established and conducted at the school media center:

1. **Print material.** Spine and jacket repairs, taping torn pages and replacing processing features.
2. **Nonprint materials.** Cleaning, splicing, and repairing cases.
3. **Equipment.** Cleaning and bulb replacement.
4. **Inventory and weeding** of print and non-print materials; regular replacement of worn or outdated equipment.
5. **Recordkeeping** on items that have been lost or stolen, damaged by nature or neglect, transferred, or discarded.
6. **Security systems,** procedures for emergency disasters, and safe storage of duplicate records.

District collection development policies may be general or specific but always address areas of concern to all schools. The policy statement should reflect the philosophy of the district, indicate the legal responsibility of the school board, and the delegation of authority to specific individuals at the district and school level. One statement will usually address all instructional materials, including textbook and library media resources.

The objectives of the policy may include:

1. Providing resources containing information that supports and enhances the school's curriculum.
2. Providing resources appropriate to users' needs, abilities, and learning styles.
3. Providing resources that develop literary appreciation and artistic values.
4. Providing resources reflecting the cultural and ethnic diversity of society and the contributions of members of various groups to our country's heritage.
5. Providing materials that enable students to solve problems and make judgments relevant to real life.
6. Providing resources that present opposing views on historical or contemporary issues, so that students may learn to think critically and objectively.

District plans may deal with:

1. Funding policies.
   a. **Allocation.** School media centers generally receive a portion of the general operating budget. The total amount is determined by a per-student dollar amount and may come directly from the district media accounts or, under school-based management, may be apportioned from school budget categories.
   b. **Authorization for purchases.** These policies vary depending on who has control of the budget: principal, district or media supervisor, district purchasing agent or any combination of the three. In some districts purchase requests must also be approved by curriculum supervisors.
   c. **Supplemental sources.** Federal or state block grants, endowments, or district capital outlay funds are allocated on a per-capita or special-project basis. Responsibility for preparation of grant applications is supervised or conducted at the district level. Some districts also set policy concerning the suitability of private donations of materials or equipment.
2. **Preview of considered materials.** Some districts seek total control of previewing.
3. **Collection size.** Districts will frequently set minimum materials and equipment levels, especially if they aim to meet regional accreditation standards.
4. **Resource sharing.** Some decisions concerning delivery systems, cooperative funding, software licensing, and liability are determined by the district.
5. **Time constraints.** All districts require that funds be expended by a specific deadline.
6. **District media library policies and procedures.** Materials that are either too expensive for school budgets and will be used by more than one school are maintained at the district library.
7. **Maintenance and repair of equipment and materials.** Districts maintain repair contracts and set procedures for their use. Annual inventories, especially of equipment, are required.
8. **Central processing.** Available in some districts, this department processes materials for convenience and uniformity.

Challenges to materials. From time to time libraries will receive challenges regarding the content of library resources. It is important for schools to have a reconsideration policy for challenged books. According the American Library Association's (ALA) Library Bill of Rights, libraries are sources of information that should cover all points of view on all topics following the rules of The First Amendment. The association does not believe that information should be removed from the library for any reason if it fits the criteria of the selection policy.

Despite the best collection development policies, an occasional complaint will arise. In our society the following issues are frequent sources of controversy: politics, gay rights, profanity, pornography, creationism vs. evolution, the occult, sex education, racism, and violence. Adults disagree philosophically about these issues. They will often express their concern first to the school library media specialist, who is ethically bound to protect intellectual freedom, but is also bound by those same principles to treat the complaint seriously as the expression of an opposing view.

The most important thing is not to panic. The challenge is not an affront to the media specialist but a complaint about the content, language, or graphics in a material. The first step is to greet the complainant calmly and explain the principles of intellectual freedom you are bound to uphold. A good paraphrase from the AECT Statement is that a learner's right to access information can only be abridged by an agreement between parent and child. With the current emphasis on the V chip for selective television viewing, parents are becoming more aware of their own roles in censoring unwanted images from their children.

In most instances a calm, rational discussion will satisfy the challenger.

However, if the challenge is pursued, the media specialist will have to follow district procedures for handling the complaint. The appropriate school administrator should be informed. Of course, an administrator may have been confronted initially. In either instance the complainant is asked to fill out a formal complaint form, citing his specific objection in a logical manner. Sometimes, simply thinking the issue through clearly and recognizing that someone will truly listen to the complaint is enough of a solution. If all else fails, a reconsideration committee should be appointed to take the matter under advisement and recommend a course of action.

Many school districts have a reconsideration policy in place. If a district does not, a good place to go for assistance is the ALA website. Here are a few things to consider.

1. Develop a statement of principles for your library that expresses the school's position on access to information. The Library Bill of Rights will be a good reference for the wording of such a statement.
2. Outline a procedure for handling the challenged material. This could include:
    a. Notifying the principal when a challenge arises
    b. Procedures to follow if the complaint cannot be resolved informally
    c. Provision of forms to file for formal complaints
    d. Responsibilities of the library advisory committee
    e. Procedures for notifying the person filing the complaint of the reconsideration committee's decision.
3. It is important to lay out the responsibilities of the school-level reconsideration committee so that it will understand the procedures for handling the complaint.

Skill 8.3 Applying procedures for working collaboratively with others to identify the needs of students; plan purchases; and design, develop, and evaluate resources

Justifications for having a school library media advisory committee include:

1. All groups affected by the library media program are given an opportunity to provide input during the planning, implementation, and evaluation process.
2. A cooperative plan ensures that all participants accept and promote the program.
3. A committee-directed plan, though slower in completion, alleviates the burden of decision making of the media specialist.

No specific guidelines exist for the organization of a library media advisory committee. However, representation from administration, faculty, student body, and parents is essential. The number of participants is affected by the size of the student body and the extent of parental involvement. In elementary schools with active PTAs there may be as many parents as teachers. In secondary schools, where parents take a less active role in their children's education, the committee may struggle to find one parent. Students may be nominated by the faculty, may volunteer, or may be members of a student government subcommittee. Each grade level or content area should have teacher representation. The principal should serve or designate a representative.

The role of leader usually falls to the media specialist, though an elected adult chairperson who is not a media specialist is preferable. It is too easy in some schools for the committee to merely rubber-stamp the decisions and actions of the media specialist, who does all the work.

The responsibilities of a library media advisory committee may include:

1. Collection development.
    a. Decisions about the purchase of audiovisual equipment and computer hardware and software.
    b. Assisting with collection weeding.
    c. Reviewing challenged material.
2. Program planning.
    a. Reviewing policies and procedures.
    b. Setting priorities.
    c. Allocating the budget.
3. Operation (volunteering).
    a. Teaching information skills.
    b. Raising funds, especially through book fairs.
    c. Producing promotional materials, such as bulletin boards, newsletters, and manuals.
4. Evaluation: preparing and tabulating results of needs assessment surveys.

Conveniently scheduled meetings should be held regularly, with a specific agenda and minutes. Problem-solving plans with specific, attainable goals should be followed by implementation of the solution. Reports of meetings should be communicated to students, teachers, and parent groups.

Skill 8.4 Applying procedures for communicating with and involving the learning community in the evaluation, selection, and deselection processes

It is important to ensure that the resources in the school library's collection are current and meets the needs of the students. One way to accomplish this is by mapping the collection.

Collection mapping is the practice of examining the quantity and quality of your resource collection. A collection map will provide a graphic display of the extent of the collection. In other words, the collection map offers a quick snapshot of the collection.

The collection should be divided into three areas:

1. A base or core collection that provides something for everyone.
2. General-emphasis collections that cover curricular needs in specific subjects and grade levels.
3. Specific-emphasis collections that cover the needs of particular units or topics.

Collection maps have many benefits. These include:

1. Identifying strengths and weaknesses within the collection.
2. Determining whether the resources match the curriculum and state standards.
3. Planning for purchases.
4. Identifying sections in need of weeding.

Since school libraries are sources of information for staff and students, it is important that the information be current and relevant. While most schools have a selection policy it is also important to have a weeding policy. Weeding the collection requires the school library media specialist to remove outdated information or worn books from the shelves.

There are many resources that provide assistance with weeding procedures. A few things to take into consideration when reviewing your collection for weeding are:

1. Weeding should be an ongoing process.
2. Books should be reviewed for currency, frequency of use, condition, multiple copies, and accuracy of information.
3. Suggested weeding procedures for each Dewey level are:

   000: Encyclopedias every five years, other materials no more than eight years
   100: Every five to eight years.
   200: Religious books can have a high turnover; keep them current.
   300: Replace almanacs every two years and keep political information current.
   400: Check for wear and tear frequently.
   500: Continuously update to make sure scientific information is current.
   600: Continuously update medical information, as older information can be misleading or dangerous.
   700: Keep until worn.
   800: Keep until worn.
   900: Weed about every two years.
   Biography: Keep the most current or best written titles.
   Fiction: Weed for multiple copies, keep those that are in best shape and have the most literary value.
   Reference: Weed for currency and accuracy.

Skill 8.5 **Analyzing issues and considerations related to the selection of resources and equipment for a school library media program (e.g., intellectual freedom, copyright, specialized collection development, accessibility, avoidance of bias) and using professional selection tools When selecting resources for a school library media program, the media specialist must follow particular guidelines and principles.**

One of the first things to consider is the principles of intellectual freedom. School library media specialists must provide resources that cover a wide range of information types and sources. From there the media specialist arms students with strategies to find, judge and use the information to meet their needs.

A crucial task for the school library media specialist is to provide access to information. Some titles may be acquired in different formats. For example, a book may be acquired in print, audio, and video.

Special collections that focus on particular curricular topics may be needed to enhance support for a particular unit. Many of these purchases are requested by specific grade levels or subjects when the collection is found to be insufficient for the needs of the course.

Skill 8.6 Demonstrating knowledge of considerations involved in collection analysis (e.g., balance, alignment with curriculum and learning, representation of diversity, age of collection)

By conducting a collection analysis, the school library media specialists can obtain a clear picture of the state of their resources.

The first step in the process is to extract circulation information from the school's automated circulation system. Gather the number of resources found in various Dewey classification areas to see if the numbers available meet local and state curricular needs. Use the system to pull a list of books with copyright dates prior to a specific year in time-sensitive areas such as science and technology. These materials may need to be discarded. The frequency of use of particular resources is another piece of helpful information when conducting a collection analysis.

Another step in the process of collection analysis is to browse the shelves to check for books that may be worn or in need of repair. Physically browsing the books allows the media specialist to become more familiar with the collection. In addition to checking the wear and tear of the books this is very helpful in determining how appealing the collection is to patrons. One cannot underestimate the power of an eye-catching book.

Another useful step in conducting a collection analysis may include surveying staff and students to determine whether or not the collection meets their needs based on interest or curricular topics.

One of the final determiners of the status of a collection is to measure it against local, state, and national guidelines for media collections for particular grade levels.

SUBAREA III. INFORMATION LITERACY SKILLS

COMPETENCY 0009 UNDERSTAND METHODS OF TEACHING INFORMATION SKILLS TO STUDENTS.

Skill 9.1 Using knowledge of child development and pedagogy to provide students with age-appropriate information sources and instructional strategies and services

Providing relevant information based on the developmental needs of the student population is important for any school library media program.

Younger students require resources that will stimulate their desire to learn to read and become lifelong learners. These resources need to support language development and provide them a chance to interact with their world.

Older elementary students are building fluency. They need materials that are of personal interest as well as meet their academic requirements.

Middle and high school age students are trying to find their place in the world. They need materials that inspire and motivate them academically, materials that are of personal interest, and resources that can help them make informed decisions to become 21st century citizens.

Each student is different. It is crucial that school library media centers provide a collection of resources that will fulfill the needs of the student population it serves.

Skill 9.2 Demonstrating understanding of various approaches to an information-seeking process

Information literacy can be defined as the capability to understand when information is needed and to identify, evaluate, and use the information effectively. It combines what we have known for years with the skills needed to thrive in the future. With the increased access to information that is possible because of technology, it is crucial for learners to not only be able to locate information but to distinguish between that which is valid and that which is not.

There are many models of information literacy. One of the most commonly used is the Big6 model. It was created by educators Mike Eisenberg and Bob Berkowitz. The Big6 process outlines how people solve an information problem.

They have broken down this process into six stages.

1. **Task Definition:** Identifying the problem and the information needed.
2. **Information Seeking Strategies**: Deciding on sources of information and selecting the best.
3. **Location and Access:** Locating the sources and searching for the information.
4. **Use of Information:** Interacting with the information and picking out that which is most relevant.
5. **Synthesis:** Organizing and presenting the information.
6. **Evaluation:** Evaluate the effectiveness of the product and the process.

Another popular model includes Pathways to Knowledge Information Skills Model, created by Marjorie Pappas and Ann Tepe. This model outlines strategies that include appreciation, pre-search, search, interpretation, communication, and evaluation.

Skill 9.3   Evaluating differentiated teaching strategies for encouraging critical and creative thinking and developing information literacy skills (e.g., reading skills, listening skills, viewing skills)

Critical thinking skills are essential in the stand against students simply accepting the information presented to them. You will introduce and develop the critical thinking skills in your school's students, providing them the tools to question not only the assumptions of others, but also their own ideas, thoughts, and established opinions.

Too many students prefer to passively absorb information without questioning its origin, usefulness, bias, or purpose. Without critical thinking skills, it's unlikely these students will have high retention of the material they learn.

Critical thinking skills develop from even the simplest of tasks assigned to students. Any assignment that asks children to make a choice or state an opinion is an exercise in critical thinking.

Encourage activities such as group discussion, summary writing, identifying the central idea or question in the topic studied, or drawing conclusions using supporting evidence. Encourage statements of opinion, assumptions, or observation. You will find that students respond differently to various instructional methods, which is why it is important to have a full arsenal of critical thinking skill activities available.

Work with the teachers to develop and coordinate ongoing critical thinking activities, such as having students research and present both sides of a topic. Encourage the exploration of questions phrased at an age-appropriate level, such as "What do I think about this topic? Why? What more would I wish to learn? How did I arrive at my conclusion or observation?"

Skill 9.4 **Selecting and adapting strategies and resources, including new and adaptive technologies, to assist students with diverse learning abilities, styles, and needs**

Schools today serve a very diverse population of students, including those from various cultures and socioeconomic backgrounds, and those with physical and learning disabilities. It is of the utmost importance that the school library media programs provide resources and technologies that help all students gain access to information.

Resources must come in a wide variety of formats, including large-print books, audio books, video books, and Braille.

Technology has made it easier for students with physical and learning disabilities to learn. Software such as the Kurzweil Reader can read scanned pages or online text to students with reading difficulties. There are many devices that help students with limited language abilities or mobility. These types of devices are called assistive or adaptive technology.

Assistive technology includes any device that helps someone with a disability perform a task that might otherwise be impossible. These devices can include: joysticks, keyboard overlays or extensions, optical pointing devices, touch screens, Braille displays and embossers, and screen enhancement.

School library media specialists teach all children within a school. It is important that the resources be available so that every child is successful.

Skill 9.5 **Recognizing ways to assist students seeking information for personal interest and self-improvement and to promote independent learning opportunities that address various learning styles**

This objective can be best achieved if there are existing scope and sequences in other curricular areas. Information skills, like any other content, should not be taught in isolation if they are to be retained and practiced. If no printed sequential exists, consult with teachers and/or team leaders about planning activities cooperatively to teach information and content skills concurrently.

Teaming with teachers helps them meet their instructional objectives. Media specialists need to match resources to those objectives and suggest means for using media to demonstrate students' mastery of skills. The design of resource-based teaching units with supplemental or total involvement of the library media center's resources and services satisfies levels 9 and 10 of Loertscher's eleven-level taxonomy. This assumes the active involvement of the school library media specialist in the total school program.

Finally, the self-esteem of students and teachers who learn information management skills is as significant as the information acquisition.

A suggested procedure for incorporation follows:

Preparation:

1. Secure any printed scope and sequences from content areas.
2. Meet with team leaders or department chairs early in the year to plan an integrated, sequential program.
3. Attend department or grade-level meetings with specific time devoted to orienting teachers to available resources and services.
4. Plan best time to schedule orientations for entry level students and reviews for reinforcement.

Implementation:

1. Conduct planned lessons. Distribute copies of objectives, activities, and resources.
2. Review search strategies and challenge students to broaden the scope of resources used to locate information.
3. Provide adequate time for students to carry out lesson activities using media center resources.

Evaluation:

1. Solicit feedback from both students and teachers.
2. Incorporate suggestions into lesson plans.

The International Society of Technology in Education has developed National Educational Technology Standards (NETS) that outline information literacy skills.

To summarize these skills:

- Student should have quick and easy access to information.
- Students should learn to be critical evaluators of information.
- Students should be able to utilize information resourcefully.

Skill 9.6   Demonstrating knowledge of national information literacy standards and guidelines

The American Association of School Librarians and the Association for Educational Computing and Technology have established national guidelines for information literacy. They can be found chapter 2 of the publication, *Information Power: Building Partnerships for Learning*.

These standards provide specific skills and rubrics that students who are information-literate should possess. Information-literate students should be able to access, evaluate and use information correctly. Information literate students pursue, appreciate and strive for excellence in searching for information. Information literate students are responsible citizens with regards to information.

COMPETENCY 0010 UNDERSTAND HOW TO DETERMINE INFORMATION NEEDS AND INITIATE SEARCHES AND HOW TO TEACH THESE SKILLS TO STUDENTS.

Skill 10.1 Applying procedures for formulating essential questions of problems and designing information search plans

Essential questions are at the top of the Bloom's Taxonomy scale. They involve the highest level of thinking. Essential question allow the student to search for deeper meanings and expand to allow further questioning to occur.

Good essential questions are open-ended and focus on broad themes or topics. Key points to consider when forming essential questions include:

- Think about the unit or information that will be covered and its key objectives.
- Utilize ideas that come from students that center around particular topics or their interests.
- Review local or state standards.
- Examine a particular learning theme from the curriculum

To form the questions have the students brainstorm possible questions that would cause them to think deeply about the topic. Try to phrase the question so that it does not influence their thinking by avoiding such words as good or bad.

Skill 10.2 Evaluating potential sources of information with regard to specific criteria (e.g., currency, format, authority, accuracy, bias, coverage)

As students begin to search for information resources for research or other projects it is important to evaluate the resources selected for their effectiveness.

There are several key factors to consider when looking at any type of resource be it a book or web page.

These criteria include:

1. **Audience.** Whom was this information intended to reach? What is the level of the information?
2. **Scope.** How detailed is the information? Is this work focused on an overall outline of the topic or does it provide in depth information on one specific aspect of the topic?
3. **Currency.** When was the information published? How often is the website updated?
4. **The author.** Who is the author? What authority does this person have to be writing this article?
5. **Objectivity.** Is the article free from bias? Is it from a single person or an organization trying to argue for a certain position?

6. **Sources.** Does the author include a bibliography of sources consulted?
7. **Intellectual level.** Does the information come from a scholarly or popular publication?

Skill 10.3   **Recognizing ways of structuring searches across a variety of sources and formats to locate the best information for a particular need**

Whether searching for information in print indices or electronic resources, it is necessary to formulate strategies for locating information prior to beginning a search to save time and effort.

One of the first things that must be determined is the specific topic that is being researched. Narrow this down to the most specific term possible. This term will be the keyword for the search.

In print references it can be helpful to consult an index to locate the keyword or any cross-referenced topics.

Electronic resources offer a wider array of strategies for locating information. Two of the most common strategies are:

Boolean operators:

- **AND:** Both words must be found in the searched text. Example: Lions AND tigers.
- **AND NOT:** The first term must be found, but not the second. Example: Lions AND NOT tigers.
- **OR:** Either term must be found. Example: Lions OR tigers.

Wildcards are an effective tool if one is unsure of the spelling or date of the search topic. An example would include the search for a list of all words in a database beginning with the letters **phil**. In many databases a search for **phil***. The asterisk at the end causes the search to retrieve records in the database that contain any word beginning with those letters.

Skill 10.4 **Applying strategies for eliciting information needs from learners (e.g., identifying the type of information needed, placing information needs in a frame of reference, relating the information to prior knowledge)**

Reference requests are of three types depending on the depth of the question and the scope of the search. Some very simple questions can lead to complex searches, however.

1. **Ready reference request.** These requests usually require a limited search in standard reference books (encyclopedias, atlases, almanacs, etc.) or electronic databases (SIRS Researcher, Grolier's Encyclopedia, 3D Atlas, or American Heritage Dictionary and Thesaurus). The request is satisfied by directing the requestor to the exact sources in which the information may be found. Occasionally, a seemingly simple question cannot be answered quickly and thus necessitates a higher level search.
2. **Ready reference for biographies.** If the library carries the *Who's Who in America* and *Who Was Who in America* series, an American is easy to identify. However, most school library media centers do not purchase biographical dictionaries of foreign persons unless they were noteworthy in a particular profession. *Who's Who in Science, Current Biography, Webster's Biographical Dictionary, British Writers Before 1900,* etc. are some helpful resources.
3. **Specific need requests.** These requests are the most frequently addressed and may range from merely steering the requestor to a library catalog, index, or other bibliographic aid if the user is familiar with those tools. It may become a lengthy project if the resource must be found outside the school or if the user needs instruction in using search tools and locating the resources. For example, a student debater may want to know which resources would give statistics about teen pregnancy. A teacher may ask which books and periodicals have the best articles on inclusion of special education students. The answer to specific need questions entails locating the resources by identifying the proper search tools, such as the library catalog or periodical indexes.
4. **Research request.** This question is encountered most often in secondary school or university/academic libraries. The search is broader in scope and requires more time. Any specific need request could be expanded into a research request. For example, the debater may be preparing a portfolio for contest and need photocopies of available material. A teacher taking a college course may ask the school library media specialist to pull periodical articles relating to inclusion. These requests may require using sources outside the library media center. Demand for research services is increasing as users are confronted with great amounts of information and have less time to conduct their searches.

COMPETENCY 0011 UNDERSTAND HOW TO LOCATE AND ACCESS RESOURCES AND HOW TO TEACH THESE SKILLS TO STUDENTS

Skill 11.1 Identifying key words, subject headings, and cross-references for searches

When searching for information the researcher first begins with the topic. Write down words or phrases that directly related to the topic being covered. Start with general terms and then break it down into more specific areas. These terms become the keywords that will be used in the search. A keyword is an important word or phrase that is used to retrieve information.

Once the keyword(s) has been determined, use it to search for books, articles, or electronic resources. When searching through print materials the researcher will look for specific subject headings. Subject headings are words or phrases that are used to locate resources by topics.

When information can be found under more than one subject heading the information is often cross-referenced. The words "See also" may be used to direct the researcher to a more appropriate heading.

Skill 11.2 Applying procedures for accessing information from diverse sources within and outside the library media center

With the use of technology, students are no longer limited to the resources sound specifically in the school library media center. They may conduct searches through online databases, books, and resources from other libraries. The same search strategies that can be used within the media center can be applied to outside resources.

Using Internet search engines students can search for information online. Careful consideration needs to be taken when using information found online for research purposes. Consult various evaluation techniques for determining the validity of the information.

Many sources, both free and paid, provide full-text books that can be used for research purposes. Websites such as Questia.com provide many academic titles that can be accessed for a minimal fee.

Public and academic libraries now provide access to many of its books and artifacts online. There are specific search engines and procedures for each entity. Their guidelines should be consulted before conducting extensive research.

Skill 11.3 Applying procedures for using information retrieval systems (e.g., catalogs, indices)

Utilizing information retrieval systems is very similar to searching for information in other formats. The user may need to know specific keywords, can often use Boolean Operators or even use wild cards.

Depending upon the system, researchers may need to know specific details concerning the database itself. They may need to know key database field names or categories to define their search. For example, if the school nurse needs to find health information regarding a particular student they would need to know how the name categories are arranged. If the database searches for the first and last name together the nurse may have difficulty locating the student if he/she types in only the last name.

When searching through library catalogs students may have more options than just conducting a keyword search. To narrow a search, books may be searched by author or title. In some instances the search could involve locating materials on a particular reading level.

When conducting any search it helps if the researcher is somewhat familiar with the capabilities and/ or limitations of the resource being used.

Skill 11.4 Recognizing ways of helping students develop skills and independence in locating and accessing resources

For students to be truly information literate they need to be armed with strategies that will guide them through the abundance of resources they are able to access. Their independence evolves as they:

- Learn to develop essential questions (See 10.1).
- Identify the keywords needed to locate information (See 11.1).
- Apply various search strategies to find information (See 10.3, 11.3, 11.2).
- Evaluate the information that is found (See 10.2).
- Find creative ways to share their information.

COMPETENCY 0012 UNDERSTAND STRATEGIES FOR ASSESSING PROGRESS DURING A SEARCH, ANALYZING AND EVALUATING INFORMATION, AND TEACHING THESE SKILLS TO STUDENTS.

Skill 12.1 Recognizing ways of evaluating the progress of a search

When conducting a search for information it is necessary to review the results carefully to ensure proper records are being returned. This is especially true for online searches.

Once results from a search have been received the user should examine their findings. Did the search return too few records or too many? Are the records relevant to the topic being searched?

After the results have been examines the search may need to be adjusted using the steps found in skill 12.2.

Skill 12.2 Determining appropriate adjustments to search strategies and evaluating whether expected outcomes of a search were achieved

When conducting a search it may be necessary to modify search strategies or parameters in order to narrow the results or to find more relevant information. One of the first places to begin is by analyzing the results that have been returned. Are their certain irrelevant references that continuously appear in the search? Are references relevant to the search topic appearing?

Three types of results require modification of the search strategy: the user retrieves too many records, too few records, or no relevant records.

When too many records are returned, the user may need to narrow the topic or make it more specific. Using Boolean strategies to eliminate irrelevant hits can make a difference. Another strategy is to put key phrases in quotation marks so that the terms would be listed together.

When a search returns too few records, it may be necessary to broaden the search. The search may have been too narrow. Take a look at any relevant records that were retrieved and examine the descriptors and keywords to locate potential terms to add to the search.

If no relevant records are returned, check the spelling of the search topic or look for the information in a different source.

Skill 12.3 Applying criteria for evaluating information (e.g., determining authority, distinguishing fact from opinion, comparing information for difference sources)

The World Wide Web has brought information directly to the end- user. With such an abundance of information it is important to teach students and adults how to discriminate the good from the bad. When looking at online information there are key points to consider.

1. How accurate is the information?
2. Who wrote the information? What authority do they have on the subject?
3. What type of site is it: commercial (.com), organizational (.org), or educational (.edu)?
4. How current is the information?
5. Is it easy to navigate or does it require special software to load?

Skill 12.4 Evaluating the effectiveness of information presented in various formats

When presenting information to a group it is important to take into consideration the objective of the presentation, the audience who will be receiving the information, as well as the location. This will determine the level at which the information should be shared, the duration of the presentation, and the best format to use.

To determine the effectiveness of the presentation simple evaluations can be conducted:

1. Observe reaction of audience to resources. Body language and verbal reactions, especially in younger children, will indicate the level of interest.
2. Solicit verbal or written reactions to appearance, arrangement, and technical quality as well as ease of understanding and mastery of content.
3. Examine costs. Determine if costs of materials and time invested were equal to outcomes.

Skill 12.5 Applying skills for summarizing, organizing, and synthesizing information

Bloom's Taxonomy reminds us that students need to develop higher level thinking skills, those skills beyond the basic recalling of facts. It is important for students to understand how to work with information once it is received. Three key skills must be in place.

The first is the ability to summarize. By summarizing information students show that they have comprehended the material and can restate key facts. This is the second level of Bloom's Taxonomy.

A little further up the scale is organizing information. The student takes the information presented and begins to categorize, compare, and contrast it. Organization is found at level 4 of Bloom's list under Analysis.

The next step on the scale is the synthesis of information. This is the second highest level, Evaluation being the highest. When information is synthesized it is collected, developed, and further organized so that it can be used for creating a product.

Skill 12.6　Applying methods of helping students evaluate and interpret information (e.g., determining whether information whether information addresses the original problem, drawing conclusions from information obtained in a search)

Evaluation revolves around a student's ability to judge the value of information. The evaluation is to be based on specific criteria. The criteria may focus on the organization of information, the relevance of the information, or criteria defined by the learning activity itself.

The evaluation may involve the use of a rubric. A rubric is a scoring guide for projects, which may be subjective. The rubric outlines specific criteria for a project. Students can determine how well they have met the criteria or answered their essential question.

When the project involves specific bits of information used to try and prove a point or complete an experiment, students can analyze the results to see if the information they gathered met their needs. By interpreting information, students can draw conclusions and begin to take a specific position or determine potential outcomes based upon their information.

COMPETENCY 0013 UNDERSTAND HOW TO COMMUNICATE INFORMATION OBTAINED FROM A SEARCH AND HOW TO TEACH THIS SKILL TO STUDENTS.

Skill 13.1 Applying guidelines for preparing a bibliography or works-cited list

Citing resources used for research or student projects is an important part of teaching students about copyright and fair use of information. When citing resources it is best to follow the preferred format of the instructor. There are many online tools that can assist students with this process. The tools generally follow one of the following types of bibliographic formats are:

- **MLA: Modern Language Association style**
  1. In text, list the author's last name and page number in parentheses: (Smith 56).
  2. Works cited are listed alphabetically by the author's last name in the following format:
  Smith, John. *Book Title: Book Subtitle*. Location: Publisher, 2008.
- **APA: American Psychological Association style**
  1. In text, when the author is not mentioned, a citation reads:
  (Smith, 2008, p. 56). When the author is mentioned, the abbreviated citation in text would read: (2008, p. 56).
  2. The reference listing is:
  Smith, J. (2008). Book title: Book subtitle. Location: Publisher.
- **Chicago Manual of Style**
  1. In text, list the author's last name and publication date: (Smith 2008).
  2. The bibliography entry is:
  Smith, John. 2008. Book title: Book subtitle. Location: Publisher.

Skill 13.2 Organizing information into a form that clearly communicates what has been learned

Planning:

1. **State the main idea** (goal) of the production, clearly and concisely.
2. **Determine the purpose** of the product.
   a. To provide information or develop appreciation. Media with this purpose is general in nature, usually meant for presentation to a class or larger group, and involves the audience as passive listeners. However, it must use dramatic or motivational appeals to hold audience interest.
   b. To provide instruction. Designed for individual or small group use, instructive media should be specific, systematic, and interactive.
3. **Develop the objectives.** State specifically what the audience should know or be able to do after using this media and what measurements will be used to determine their knowledge or ability.

4. **Analyze the audience.** Determine ability and interest, learning styles, and current understanding of the topic.
5. **Research the idea.** Use print, non-print, and human resources to study both the subject matter and the media techniques/formats to best present the subject matter.

Designing:

1. **Prepare an outline of the content.** Create storyboard cards for each subheading and match them to the objectives.
2. **Select the media format(s)** to communicate your idea. Consider time, effort, and cost as well as audiovisual needs. If motion or sound is not essential, consider using transparencies or slides, which are easier to make and require no editing. Consider the equipment and facilities available.
3. **Create the content.** Prepare a storyboard delineating the description of each graphic and write a corresponding script if captions or sound narration will be included.
4. **Create the media** (3.4.4).

Evaluating:

1. **Observe reaction** of audience to resources. Body language and verbal reactions, especially in younger children, will indicate the level of interest.
2. **Solicit verbal or written reactions** to appearance, arrangement, and technical quality as well as ease of understanding and mastery of content.
3. **Examine costs.** Determine whether costs of materials and time invested were equal to outcomes.

Skill 13.3   Applying procedures for selecting an appropriate format to communicate information (e.g., print, audio, video, multimedia) and for producing an effective end product

Many excellent books on media instruction detail the instructional uses of media formats. A few will be summarized here.

1. Formats that allow large group listening or viewing are appropriate for introducing new materials: computer projection, overhead transparencies, audio and video in various formats. These require large screen, elevation of monitor, or multiple units. With young learners display boards with large print and audiocassettes for storytelling with nonreaders are most effective.
2. When students are learning to apply a particular skill, media that lend themselves to individual or small group use are needed. As students investigate the subject matter, organize that information, practice, or demonstrate understanding, they may create any or several types of media. With young children these include manipulatives: building blocks, letters or numbers, or shapes in cloth, plastic, or wood. Older students create photographs/slides, audio recordings, or video. Some secondary students may even design their own computer programs. Students at all levels can be taught to use computer design software to create multimedia productions.

Skill 13.4   Applying methods for helping students think creatively about approaches to and formats for communicating information

The application of media production techniques helps the producers, whether adults or children, to clarify their own objectives and determine the exact format that would best present their ideas and achieve their goals. A lesson on distinguishing the calls of local birds might use audio recording while recognition of plumage uses slides or video. Students preparing a study of estuarine ecology might incorporate video and computer graphics designed from electron microscope imagery to demonstrate types of microorganisms in the local river.

TEACHER CERTIFICATION STUDY GUIDE

SUBAREA IV.   **PROGRAM ADMINISTRATION AND LEADERSHIP**

COMPETENCY 0014   **UNDERSTAND THE LEADERSHIP ROLE OF THE LIBRARY MEDIA SPECIALIST WITHIN THE ENTIRE EDUCATIONAL COMMUNITY**

Skill 14.1   **Applying strategies for participating in district, building, department, and grade-level curriculum design and assessment projects to ensure that the library media program is integral to the school curriculum**

School library media specialists should be more involved in curriculum planning than current research indicates, both on school and district curriculum teams. Sometimes principals must be coaxed into including school library media professionals in curriculum planning because they occasionally forget that media professionals are teaching professionals. The school library media specialist must volunteer to participate and hope that the administration places a value on the contribution she has to offer.

As a team member, the school library media specialist contributes by:

1. Advising on current trends and studies in curriculum design.
2. Advising the school staff on the use of media and instructional techniques to meet learning objectives.
3. Ensuring that a systematic approach to instruction in information skills is included in curriculum plans.
4. Recommending media and technologies appropriate to particular subject matter and activities.

Instructional planning for the school library media specialist is the process of effectively integrating library skills instruction into the curriculum.

Methods of instructional planning:

1. Identifying content. Teachers create a list of instructional objectives for specific classes. Library media specialists, using state and local scope and sequence, prepare a list of objectives for teaching information skills.
2. Specifying learning objectives. Teachers and library media specialists working together should merge the list of objectives
3. Examining available resources.
4. Determining instructional factors:
   a. Learner styles.
   c. Teaching techniques and division between teacher and library media specialist division of responsibilities for lesson implementation.
   d. Student groupings. Consider abilities, special needs, etc.
5. Pretest.
6. Determining activities to meet objectives.

LIBRARY & MEDIA SPECIALIST

7. Selecting specific resources and support agencies.
8. Implementation of the unit.
9. Evaluation.
10. Revision of the objectives and activities.

Skill 14.2   Applying advocacy strategies to build support for the library media program among teachers, administrators, school board members, parents/guardians, students, and the community

Building support for the school library media program creates a network of individuals willing to work to enhance the students' learning experiences. It all begins with a program mission that supports advocacy.

The American Library Association has developed an Advocacy Toolkit to assist libraries in promoting their programs. It includes:

- **@ Your Library** program outlines the role of the school library media specialists and the programs they manage.
- PowerPoint presentations that explain **@ Your Library** and provide topics of discussion.
- Implementation plan for Information Power.
- Brochures for promoting advocacy.
- Guides for meeting with government officials.
- Resource guides for promoting the media center, intellectual freedom and other topics.
- Communication handbook.

> Learn more about @ Your Library
>
> http://www.ala.org/ala/proftools/21centurylit/21stcenturyliteracy.htm

Skill 14.3   Applying procedures for establishing partnerships with the school community to support learning objectives, share the vision of the library media program, and engage in long-range, strategic planning

The school library media program is no longer an isolated entity within a school. One of the most valuable things they can do to promote the library media program is to develop partnerships within the community. Research has shown that strong parental and community involvement can increase student achievement.

When considering the formation of partnerships, the school library media specialist must first examine the curriculum for the grade levels the center serves, as well as the goals for the media program. This will help to determine the people, agencies, and organizations that will best help meet student needs.

To begin the process, the school library media specialist must contact the agency to see what possible programs they have available for students. An explanation of the particular curriculum needs will help determine whether the agency is willing to provide any needed services or resources.

Reasons for partnerships include:

- Location of additional programs or resources to expand student learning experience.
- Financial support for library or school projects.
- Location of sites off campus where the library may hold special programs to support curricular needs.
- Greater involvement of the school library media specialist in community school-improvement efforts.
- Better knowledge of concerns and issues within the community as a whole and their impact on the school.

Skill 14.4   Demonstrating knowledge of ways to incorporate the library media program in educational reform

Until the passage of the Elementary and Secondary Education Act in 1965, which encouraged the evolution of school libraries into library media centers, school libraries were repositories of print material, mainly reference books and fiction. School librarians, who rarely had support staff, had to manage circulation and processing of materials, supervise student behavior in the library, maintain the collection, and distribute limited equipment. The explosion of information and the retrieval systems for accessing that information has revolutionized the role of the school library media specialists (3.0) and the program they oversee (1.2). Studies in child development by Jean Piaget, Erik Erikson and Lawrence Kohlberg had begun to affect collection development in post-World War II America. Learning style theories from Abraham Maslow's hierarchy to Howard Gardner's seven intelligences have modified classroom teaching.

As libraries began to evolve into full service media centers and school media specialists became instructional consultants to teachers, all aspects of program development were influenced by the need to know the factors that influence children's learning. The ability to assess the student users' needs for the media center's services and resources has become a collaborative effort with classroom teachers, who have daily contact with their students. This resulted in the move to cooperative planning and cooperative learning in the 1990's.

In the 1980's legislative actions at the national and state level (1.1), government concern for widespread literacy, and document findings such as those in *A Nation at Risk* have all reinforced that instruction must be improved in all areas.

As a result of private publications, such as James Naisbitt's *Megatrends* and *Megatrends 2000* and research by the staff of *School Library Media Quarterly*, the need to provide more than mere access to the wealth of information affects libraries in the public and private sector. Ultimately, the school library media specialist becomes the agent through which the most aggressive change will occur.

In 1988, *Information Power* was published under the supervision of AASL president, Karen Whitney, and AECT president, Elaine Didier. In the same year *Taxonomies of the School Library Media Program* by David Loertscher, senior acquisitions editor for Libraries Unlimited, appeared. There is now a considerable body of excellent reference material on school library media.

COMPETENCY 0015 UNDERSTAND FACILITIES USE IN THE LIBRARY MEDIA CENTER

Skill 15.1 Analyzing factors to be considered when designing and furnishing a library media center (e.g., efficient use of space; areas needed for specific purposes; age-appropriateness; providing accommodations for technology and for students with special developmental and educational needs; creating a warm, friendly atmosphere that is conducive to learning)

Planning for renovation or new facilities needs to be a team effort. Participants include a school-level planning committee, district-level representatives, planning consultants, the architect, and builders.

The school-level planning committee should include the school library media specialist, technology specialist, principal, teachers, students, and parents. Its responsibilities are to assist with the planning process, determine educational needs, determine technology needs, select furniture, and set priorities for the essentials needed to ensure the success of the school library media program.

There are important design elements to consider when renovating or building new facilities:

1. Traffic flow should provide easy, logical access to all spaces.
2. Security requires material detection systems, alarms or locks to protect electronic equipment, and convenient placement of communications devices.
3. Proper placement of electrical outlets, fire extinguishers, smoke detectors, and thermostats ensures safety for users and convenience for the staff.
4. Barrier-free access allows the physically impaired to access the center and its resources.
5. All areas requiring supervision should be readily visible from other areas of the center.
6. Space used for supporting activities should be carefully planned.

The specifics of spatial arrangement depend upon the types and quantities of resources and services provided. New-school design should place the media center in a central location, easily accessible to all academic areas. Within the center itself the following spatial arrangement factors should be addressed.

1. A large central area for reading, listening, viewing, and computing, with ready access to materials and equipment. AASL/AECT guidelines recommend that this main seating area be 25%-75% of the total square footage allocation, depending on program requirements. 40 sq. ft. should be allotted per student user. Within this area or peripheral to it should be smaller areas for independent study or to accommodate users with physical impairments. Seating should be adequate for the number of users during peak hours. Floor space and seating should accommodate 10% of the student body, but the media center should not be expected to seat fewer than 40 or more than 100 students at one time.
2. Areas for small- or medium-sized group activities. These areas may be acoustically special spaces adjacent to the central seating area or conference rooms, computer labs, or storytelling space. AASL/AECT recommends 1-3 areas or approximately 150 sq. ft. with ample electrical outlets, good lighting and acoustics, and a wall screen.
3. Space to house and display the collection. Circulating materials should be easily accessible from the main seating area. Index tools should be highly visible and in immediate proximity to the collections they index. A supervised circulation desk with easy access to non-circulating databases (periodicals, CD-ROM, microform, and videotape collections) should be close to the center's main entrance. AASL/AECT recommends 400 sq. ft. minimum for stacks with an additional allowance of 200 sq. ft. per 500 additional students.
4. A reference materials area within or adjacent to the central seating area. The recommended area allowance is part of the total allotted for the stacks.
5. Space for a professional collection and work area where the faculty and media professionals can work privately. This area should be approximately 1 sq. ft. per student.
6. Administrative offices, with areas for resource and equipment processing, materials duplication, and business materials storage. An area no smaller than 200 sq. ft. should be available for offices alone and double that area if in-house processing is done.
7. Equipment storage and circulation area close to administrative offices and with access to outside corridor. Space for maintenance and repair is optional depending on available staff to attend to these duties. This space should be no less than 400 sq. ft. for storage with another 150 sq. ft. if repair facilities are necessary.
8. A media production area with space and equipment for production of audio and videotaping, graphics design, photography, computer programming, and photocopying. This area may be as small as 50 sq. ft. or as large as 700 sq. ft. in a school with 500 students, depending on the amount of equipment required for production. In a school with 1,000 or more students at least 700-900 sq. ft. should be allotted for media production. In some secondary schools, a dark room is included. Schools with commercial photography classes and a full photography lab may seek services through the photography teacher.

9. A television production studio for formal TV production, class instruction, and preparation of special programming. Space for distribution of closed-circuit programs and satellite transmissions should also be provided. A 1,600 sq. ft. studio (preferably 40' x 40' x 15') should be available whenever television classes are taught or studio videotaping is a program priority. AASL/AECT guidelines allow alternatives: studio space available at the district level for the use of students, or mini-studios and portable videotape units where videotaping is done on a small scale.
10. Recommended, but optional in many schools, is a large multipurpose room adjacent to the media center for use as a lecture hall or meeting room. AASL/AECT recommends that this room be 700-900 sq. ft. in a school with 500 students (i.e. classroom size) or 900-1200 sq. ft. in a school with 1,000 students. This room should be equipped for making all types of media presentations.
11. A network/server head-end area housing network services, telephone equipment, and video distribution equipment for the entire building. The space should be 450-800 sq. ft. Equipment for this room may include network server, routers switches, telephone patch panel, cabling, and wireless devices.
12. Network access and power outlets should be available throughout the entire media center to accommodate circulation search stations, student work stations and other electronic devices.

Because of the diversity of services provided in a modern school library media center, it is important to foster a user-friendly atmosphere, one in which the patron is not only welcomed as a user of resources but is also involved as a producer of ideas and materials.

All facilities must follow provide access to those with physical handicaps. A few of the recommendations are:

1. Work surfaces at least 30" from the floor.
2. Clear aisle width for wheelchair access.
3. Large, clearly visible signs that include accommodations for the visually impaired.
4. Devices for the visually and hearing impaired. One such device is the Kurzweil reader, which reads scanned or electronic text aloud.

The library media program, in considering the academic and personal needs of the user, should provide an atmosphere in which users can attain both basic skills and enrichment goals.

Factors that influence the atmosphere include:

1. Proximity to academic classes.
2. Esthetic appearance.
3. Acoustical ceilings and floor coverings.
4. Adequate temperature control
5. Adequate, non-glare lighting with controls for different types of viewing activities.
6. Comfortable, appropriately sized, and durable furnishings.
7. Diverse, plentiful, and current resources that are attractive to handle as well as easy to use.
8. Courteous, helpful personnel, using supervisory techniques that encourage self-exploration and creativity while protecting the rules of library etiquette.

Skill 15.2   Identifying, evaluating, establishing, and using delivery systems to retrieve information in all formats and for all ability levels

Information retrieval systems are designed to help the user access information from sources such as magazines, newspapers and other documents. Some of the most widely used information retrieval systems are Internet search engines.

Automated library catalogs are also considered information retrieval systems. To prepare to convert to an automated library management system there are three main questions to consider: the budget, technical considerations, and data conversion.

The options available during the conversion process are often determined by the funds available. Necessary purchases include the software, a barcode scanner for circulation, computer hardware upgrades, and technical support. Conversion of records to electronic format can be done by the media center staff or by outside agencies for a fee. It is important to have a well-defined plan before beginning the process. When in doubt, take small steps and increase as time and money allows.

Technical considerations include software, hardware and infrastructure categories. When selecting software for library management, check local or state recommendations before making any decisions. The platform (MAC or Windows) should match the computer systems most prevalent in your district. Before purchasing the software, make sure that the school's computers meet the requirements of the software and that a network infrastructure is in place to provide maximum access. District technical-support staff should be able to assist with these decisions. It will be important to ensure that technical support is provided for the automation hardware and software. This may require an extra expense, but will be money well spent, especially during the initial setup phase.

After the technical requirements are in place, it is time to begin the data conversion process. Transferring the current card catalog into electronic format can be a daunting job. Weeding the collection in advance saves time and expense by not converting titles that will be discarded.

The actual conversion of information to electronic format is the most time-consuming task. Options include inputting the data onsite or hiring a company to convert the shelflist to electronic format. Budget is generally the biggest consideration. If the choice is to convert onsite a wise investment is the purchase of MARC CD-ROMS. This will make the process move much faster. There are companies that convert the shelflist to MARC format for a rather minimal charge, considering the time it takes to enter everything by hand. Explore the possibilities of utilizing such services and determine the impact on the automation budget.

Once the shelflist has been converted to electronic format, books must be barcoded. This generally involves printing barcode stickers and placing them on each and every book. Volunteers and student helpers can make this process move quickly.

Next, all patrons need to be added into the system. This can often be done by importing data from the school's attendance management system. If not, information will need to be keyed in by hand.

Once all of the information is in, the school library media specialist needs to input such basic information such as checkout limits, circulation periods, and other basic housekeeping information.

The conversion to an automated system is a lot of work, but the benefits far outweigh the time it takes to complete the process.

Skill 15.3   Demonstrating knowledge of scheduling considerations and applying techniques for scheduling library media center resources, equipment, and space (e.g., flexible scheduling)

The issue of flexible access is especially distressing to elementary school library media specialists who are placed in the "related arts wheel," providing planning time for art, music, and physical education teachers. "Closed" or rigid scheduling, i.e. scheduling classes to meet regularly for instruction in the library, prohibits the implementation of the integrated program philosophy essential to the principles of intellectual freedom.

The AASL Position Statement on Flexible Scheduling asserts that schools must adopt a philosophy of full integration of library media into the total educational program. This integration assures a partnership of students, teachers, and school library media specialists in the use of readily accessible materials and services when they are appropriate to the classroom curriculum.

All parties in the school community (teachers, principal, district administration, and school board) must share the responsibility for flexible access.

Research on the validity of flexible access reinforces the need for cooperative planning with teachers, an objective that cannot be met if the school library media specialist has no time for the required planning sessions. Rigid scheduling denies students the freedom to come to the library during the school day for pleasurable reading and self-motivated inquiry activities vital to the development of critical thinking, problem solving, and exploratory skills. Without flexible access, the library becomes just another self-contained classroom.

Skill 15.4   Applying procedures for operating, storing, maintaining, inventorying, and securing library media resources

Resource organization systems vary from school to school, depending on such factors as user demand, storage considerations, staff limitations and preferences, and processing procedures. Some media specialists separate specific age- or reading-level collections for ease of location, especially with younger children. Audiovisual and multimedia kits may be shelved with print material if they can be circulated to all users. Visibility creates greater use, but collection security for instructional materials and equipment must also be considered. Organizational procedures should be logical and follow standardized procedures as much as possible.

The objective of organization systems:

1. **Ready access.** To make resources, regardless of format, easy to locate, a bibliographic control system must be in place. A catalog, preferably automated, should include all print and nonprint resources and equipment.
2. **Ease of circulation.** If the catalog is not automated, the media center staff should keep accurate circulation records to facilitate retrieval and inventory. If audiovisual materials or equipment are not housed near the circulation area, a paper record is necessary. For equipment not housed in the media center, location information must appear in the catalog.

Inventory is the process of verifying the collection holdings and assessing the collection's physical condition. Its purposes are:

1. To indicate lost or missing materials. Identify items for replacement.
2. To reveal strengths and weaknesses in collection. Inventory helps identify areas where numbers of materials do not reflect need.
3. To identify materials needing repair. Periodic preventive maintenance can save major repair or replacement cost.
4. To shape the process of weeding. Outdated and damaged or worn materials would be removed to maintain the integrity of the collection's reputation.

TEACHER CERTIFICATION STUDY GUIDE

Inventory procedures:

1. Specify when inventory will be conducted. Most schools conduct inventories at the end of the school year. Many districts require the submission of inventory statistics to the school or district supervisors before media staff vacations.
2. Determine who will conduct inventory. Personnel availability determines whether inventory is conducted by professionals, support staff, or some combination, during school hours or during closed time.
3. Examine each item and match it to the holding records. Pull items for repair.
4. Tabulate results and record them on forms required by the school or district.

Skill 15.5 Recognizing policies that promote equitable access to and use library media facilities

The American Library Association promotes equitable access to resources for all patrons. Its *ADA Library Kit* provides guidelines on freedom of access for the disabled.

There are specific laws relevant to library access:

- The Rehabilitation Act of 1973 requires libraries to provide the disabled with equal access to resources.
- The Americans with Disabilities Act of 1990 also contains provisions on library access for those with disabilities. Titles II and III apply specifically to school facilities.
- The 1996 Telecommunications Act (Section 255) provides guidelines on access to computing services.

COMPETENCY 0016 UNDERSTAND PROCEDURES FOR LIBRARY MEDIA RESOURCE ORGANIZATION AND CIRCULATION

Skill 16.1 Identifying and applying standard methods of classifying and cataloging library media materials (e.g., Dewey Decimal System, Sears List of Subject Headings, U.S. MARC, AACR2, ALA filing rules)

The MARC format is relatively universal and enables a school library to utilize many commercial automation tools. It allows for unlimited fields which provide more efficient cataloging for both print and nonprint items. Each field is marked with a tag identifying a specific type of information, i.e. the 245 field gives the title and the 520 field the summary.

The MARC format assists in preserving **bibliographic integrity**, the accuracy and uniformity with which items are catalogued. Following a standard set of international rules, *Anglo-American Cataloguing Rules*, enables users to locate materials equally well in all libraries that subscribe to these rules. To maintain this integrity, catalogers:

1. Recognize an International Standard Bibliographic Description (ISBD) that establishes the order in which bibliographic elements will appear in catalog entries.
2. Note changes that occur after each five-year review of ISBD.
3. Agree to catalog all materials using the AACR standards.

The components of a basic bibliographic record in either card or electronic format include:

1. **Call Number:** A DDC or LCCN classification number followed by a book identification identifier with numerals or letters.
2. **Main Entry Heading.** Usually this is the author's name, in the form by which the author is best known. If no author is known, the title serves as main entry.
3. **Title and Statement of Responsibility Area.** Include title, subtitle, or parallel titles and name(s) of authors, editors, illustrators, translators, or groups functioning in authorship capacity.
4. **Edition Statement.** Provide ordinal number of edition.
5. **Material-Specific Details.** Used only with computer files, cartographic materials, printed music, and serials in all formats.
6. **Publication, Distribution, etc. Area.** Includes place of publication, name of publisher and copyright date.
7. **Physical Description Area.** Includes the extent of the work (number of pages, volumes, or other units); illustrative matter; size/dimensions; and accompanying materials.
8. **Series.** Provide title of series and publication information if different from statement of responsibility.

9. **Notes.** Provide information to clarify any other descriptive components, including audiovisual formats or reading levels.
10. **Standard numbers.** Provide ISBN, ISSN, or LCC number, price, or other terms of availability.

There are three levels of bibliographic description:

1. Level 1 descriptions are the simplest and most appropriate for small or general collections. Although they satisfy AACR standards, they are not considered full records.
2. Level 2 descriptions are more detailed and are used by medium to large libraries where clients use materials for research. Many libraries, including small media centers, use description format somewhere between Level 1 and Level 2.
3. Level 3 descriptions are full records that require application of every AACR rule. Most major libraries, even the Library of Congress, develop some system just short of full Level 3 cataloging.

OCLC bibliographic records (MARC) use both a short form (Level I enhanced) and a long form (Level 2).

All entries must have standardized subject headings. *Sears List of Subject Headings* is generally used in smaller libraries, while larger ones use *Library of Congress Subject Headings*.

Many companies that serve libraries provide a complete MARC records for materials ordered. This is a time-saving feature for school library media specialists.

The primary way of determining use of library materials and services is to examine circulation records. Automated systems can generate periodic circulation statistics.

Skill 16.2 Demonstrating knowledge of collection management principles and procedures

A collection of resources closely tied to the school's instructional program and the developmental and cultural needs of students is crucial to the school library media program.

To ensure the collection meets student needs there are steps the media specialist can take:

1. Stay abreast of changes in curriculum as well as the types of resources needed to meet those needs.
2. Work closely with teachers to determine resources needed.
3. Work closely with staff to determine policies and procedures.
4. Develop specific processes for evaluating and updating the collection.
5. Have access to up-to-date collection monitoring and evaluation tools and reviewing resources.
6. Support the circulation of resources by sharing information with teachers and allowing them to preview new resources as well as take part in the selection process.

Procedures for maintaining the collection are perhaps the most important in the collection plan. The plan itself must provide efficient, economical procedures for keeping materials and equipment in usable condition. On inventory, see Skill 15.4.

Maintenance policies for equipment and some policies for materials are determined at the district level. Procedures to satisfy these policies are followed at the building level.

1. Replacement or discard of damaged items based on comparison of repair to replacement cost. Districts usually maintain repair contracts with external contractors for major repairs that cannot be done at the school or district media service center.
2. Equipment inventory and records on repair or disposal. Usage records help with the transfer of usable items from school to school.
3. Book bindery contracts.

Policies and procedures for periodic inspection, preventive maintenance and cleaning, and minor repairs are established and conducted at the school media center.

1. Print material. Spine and jacket repairs, taping torn pages and replacing processing features.
2. Nonprint materials. Cleaning, splicing, repairing cases.
3. Equipment. Cleaning, bulb replacement.
4. Inventory and weeding of print and nonprint materials; regular replacement of worn or outdated equipment.
5. Record keeping on items that have been lost or stolen, damaged by nature or neglect, or transferred/discarded.
6. Security systems operation, procedures for emergency disasters, and safe storage of duplicate records.

Skill 16.3 Recognizing types of circulation patterns, controls, records, and systems and analyzing factors to be considered when establishing use and circulation policies

Circulation policies and procedures should be flexible to allow ready access and secure to protect borrowers' rights of confidentiality.

The components of circulation procedures:

1. The circulation system should:
   a. Be simple to use for the convenience of staff and to save the borrowers' time.
   b. Provide for the loan and return of print and nonprint materials and equipment.
   c. Facilitate the collection of circulation statistics.
2. Rules governing circulation include:
   a. Length of loan period.
   b. Process for handling overdues.
   c. Limitations on the number of items circulable to individual borrowers.
   d. Overnight loan for special items (vertical file materials, reference books, audio-visual materials or equipment, and reserve collections).
   e. Fines for damaged, overdue, or lost materials.
3. Security provisions
   a. Theft detection devices on print and non-print media.
   b. Straps or lock-downs on equipment transported by cart.

Automated circulation systems have several advantages.

1. Ease and speed of use.
   a. Barcodes and scanning devices speed the process.
   b. Data are quickly retrievable.
   c. Elimination of card files frees space for other uses.
2. The online catalog provides data on circulation status.
3. Collection evaluation and usage statistics.

Some disadvantages include:

1. Cost of equipment, service contracts, and annual updates.
2. Power interruptions.
3. Possible breaches of user confidentiality.

Skill 16.4 Evaluating and implementing policies to ensure equitable and reasonable access to library resources

Each school library media center should develop a policy tailored to the philosophy and objectives of that school's educational program. This policy provides guidelines by which all participants in the selection process can get insight into their responsibilities. The policy statement should reflect the following factors:

1. Compatibility with district, state, regional, and national guidelines (1.2).
2. Adherence to the principles of intellectual freedom.
3. Recognition of the rights of individuals or groups to challenge policies, procedures, or selected items and the establishment of procedures for dealing fairly with such challenges.
4. Recognition of users needs and interests, including community demographics.

Review section 15.5 for additional policies on equitable access.

TEACHER CERTIFICATION STUDY GUIDE

COMPETENCY 0017 UNDERSTAND PROCEDURES AND ISSUES RELATED TO FISCAL AND STAFF MANAGEMENT IN LIBRARY MEDIA PROGRAMS

Skill 17.1 Determining fiscal needs, setting fiscal goals, and establishing fiscal priorities for the library media program

In preparation for constructing the budget for the school library media center, the school media professionals need to consider

1. The standards set by state departments of education, local school boards, and regional accreditation associations. Changes in standards sometimes necessitate changes in local budget planning.
2. The sources of funds that support the media center program (4.3.2).
3. The prioritized list of program goals and the cost of meeting these goals.

Determining the relationship between program goals and funding involve the study of:

1. Past inventories and projections of future needs.
2. Quantitative and qualitative collection standards at all levels.
3. School and district curriculum plans.
4. Community needs.
5. Fiscal deadlines.

Skill 17.2 Applying strategies for communicating effectively within and outside the learning community about the status and needs of the library media program

Establish and nurture an administrative partnership with the principal and district director of media to develop, establish, and fund library program goals. In larger districts that have a district director of media, avenues of support may be clearly defined. In smaller districts, where the media director also handles other administrative duties or where there is no district coordinator, support is based on the lobbying efforts of the school library media specialist.

In any case, the principal must be the media center's staunchest ally. Present the annual program goals and implementation procedures to the principal early in the school year for input and approval. Invite the principal to participate in faculty in-service training and advisory committee meetings. Ask to be included on the school's curriculum planning team.

Exhibit your willingness to assume a leadership role in integrating the library media program into the total school program. Make every attempt to ensure that some phase of the library media program appears in each year's school improvement plan.

Work with the district media director and other school library media specialists to establish and maintain a uniformly excellent district library media program. Continually compare the goals and objectives of the school program to those of the district program and to the users' needs as identified in annual assessments.

Attend school board meetings. Be aware of all issues affecting the media program, instruction, and the budget. Invite county or area superintendents and school board members to district media meetings to discuss issues and plan improvements. Make yourself and your enthusiasm for the library media program visible.

A knowledgeable library media specialist is the best human resource in the school. There is perhaps no better promotion for the media center than having students, teachers, and administrators seeking information from the library media center staff.

Attend college courses, in-service training, and professional conferences. Offer to teach night college courses, supervise a library media candidate, offer workshops for school faculty, and make presentations at conferences. But, remember to be selective. Never forsake your ethical responsibility to serve patrons by overextending your commitments.

Keep apprised of state certification requirements for certificate renewal and complete renewal requirements in a timely manner.

Systematically assess program needs at least annually. Always have available statistics about media center use, lesson plans or visitation schedules, and written evaluations of instructional activities. Make presentations to school improvement committees, parent support groups, or community agencies. Thorough, accurate reports indicate a well-managed program and encourage maximum support.

Skill 17.3   Applying procedures for preparing budgets and reports, maintaining records, and running a library media program within budget

AASL/AECT guidelines identify four factors in calculating the budget for the print and nonprint collection: variation in student population, attrition by weeding, attrition by date, and attrition by loss. A formula for an estimated budget is then calculated based on points established for each of these factors. The estimation for replacement is figured on a base number of collection items required regardless of school size. The minimum collection standard is determined by the state or regional accreditation requirements.

Another method of estimating a budget for the print collection is based on the types of materials needed: replacement books, periodicals, books for growth and expansion, and reference books. It is recommended that 5% of the total books in the print collection be used in the formula.

The formula is:

5% × number of books × average cost of book = replacement cost.

For periodicals, multiply the number of periodicals by the average subscription price.

Use the following figures to calculate book collection expansion: at 90% fulfillment of basic requirement, add 3%-5%; at 75%-90% fulfillment, use 10%-15%; and at less than 75%, use 15%-25%. For reference books, multiply the number of sets times the average set price.

In a hypothetical school of 1,000-1,500 students, which seeks a collection of 10,200 books but has only 75% of that number (7650 or fewer), the expansion formula is:

15-25% × existing collection × average book price.

If our hypothetical school has 7,500 books, the formula is:

20% × 7,500 × $20 = $30,000.

If the school has 75-90% of the recommended 10,200 books, it can meet expansion guidelines by adding 10-15% of the collection. The formula is:

10% × 8,160 × $20 = $16,320.

Finally, if the school is at 90-100% of the recommendation, we expand by 3-5% or:

5% × 9690 × $20 = $9690.

Calculations for audiovisual materials follow the same basic pattern. For our school, let's assume that we have included this figure in our estimate for the print collection.

Equipment estimations are based on multiplying four elements: the current inventory replacement value; replacement of lost, stolen, or damaged items; average age of the equipment; and the inflation rate. If our hypothetical school has a current value of $200,000, the average age of items is 5 years, the average replacement cost is $200, and the inflation rate is 1.3 percent, the equipment estimation would be calculated as follows:

$200,000 x 5 = $1,000,000 x .013 = 13,000 + $200 = $13,200

The total estimated collection budget then equals the sum of estimates.

In districts in which the school library media center allocation is not calculated on local recommendations but on an across-the-board per-capita figure, the school library media specialist must work with the administration to secure necessary funds from the school budget. If funds are not categorized at the district level, the school library media specialist must set a percentage for each category based on the previously discussed factors.

When all factors have been considered, the budget process should relate the budget to the program goals and objectives. To achieve this correlation the process should follow these steps:

1. Communicate program and budget considerations to administration, faculty, students and community groups, allowing sufficient time for input from all groups.
2. Work with representatives from all groups to finalize short-range objectives and review long-range goals for use of funds.
3. Build a system of flexible encumbrance and transferal of funds as changes in needs occur.
4. As part of the program promotion, communicate budgetary concerns to all interested parties.

Skill 17.4 Demonstrating basic knowledge of local, state, federal, and private sources of funding for library media programs

Unlike public libraries, school library media centers are not usually the recipients of endowments or private gifts. School library media centers receive money from local and state tax dollars. The major portion of the funds comes from district allotments for instructional materials or capital outlays that are regulated by the state. Accredited schools must adhere to guidelines from the regional accreditation agency. The funding formulas specifically used for school library media budgets vary from district to district but basically comply with the following regulations.

1. **Local funding.** School library media centers funds are generally allocated from the district operating budget. The funds may be administered at the district or school level according to a per capita figure, adequate to meet operation costs and contractual obligations.
2. **State funds provided by special legislation.** Most special funds are in the form of block grants (funds earmarked for a specific purpose). Schools generally must apply for such funds. One example is the technology block grants that have appeared in recent years. These grants have provided funds for retrofitting schools to create local area networks, wide-area networks, and telecommunications services.
3. **Regional guidelines.** Each regional accrediting agency produces an expenditures requirement based on student body size, allowing a school to average expenditures over a three-year period in which averaged expenditures do not fall below the standard.

4. **Federal block grants** included in federal education acts (4.6.3) are awarded to states or districts and are limited in scope and time. They must be applied for on a competitive basis, and renewal depends on the recipient's ability to prove that grant objectives have been met.
5. **Federal funds earmarked for innovative technologies**, not operating costs.

In addition to official funding sources, there are other forms of assistance from the community that should be reflected in the budget plan. Because this assistance is in the form of service rather than real dollars, estimated values must be determined. Some community assistance includes

1. Partnerships with local businesses. Free wiring from cable television companies, guest speakers, distance learning opportunities, and workshops in new technologies are just a few possible services.
2. Education support groups. The education committee of the local chamber of commerce, a private education economic council, or parent associations may conduct fund-raisers or offer mini-grants.
3. 3. Corporate grants. Many large companies provide grants for specific topics such as technology, science, math and reading. The grant may involve providing equipment or funds to be used for a specific purpose.

Skill 17.5 Applying principles and procedures for selecting, supervising, and evaluating staff and for handling personnel and staffing issues

The diversity of user needs, school enrollments, and school/district support services are some factors that affect staff size. Some of the duties of different levels of staff persons overlap and differ only in the amount of decision-making and accountability.

Guidelines for school library media centers are found under the Commissioner's Regulations. Regulation 91.2 focuses on the employment of school library media specialists. Under this regulation a school district is to provide a certified school library media specialist unless the commissioner has approved a different arrangement. The standards for such an arrangement would include:

The standards for secondary schools, by size of enrollment, are:

- Less than 100 students: School library media specialist devotes at least one hour per day to library duties.
- 101-300 students: Two periods are devoted to library duties.
- 301-500 students: One-half day devoted to library duties.
- 501-700 students: Five periods devoted to library duties.
- 701-1,000 students: Entire day devoted to library duties.
- For every 1,000 students: A full-time assistant certified school library media specialist will be added for each additional 1,000 students enrolled

(Statutory authority: Education Law, § 207)

Skill 17.6 Recognizing characteristics, roles, and training needs associated with library media personnel and applying methods for conducting professional development activities for library media staff

When the support staff is reduced, the professional must assume operational duties that distract him or her from professional responsibilities. Volunteers can help with circulation and supplemental tasks that utilize their unique talents and experiences, but they should never be used as substitutes for paid clerical and technical staff.

Student assistants, like volunteers, may be trained to assist the media specialist but should not be assigned the duties of paid nonprofessionals. They might assist with production of materials, maintenance of the decoration and physical appearance of the center, instruction in materials location, use of electronic/computer databases, use or maintenance of equipment, and shelving of books and periodicals. It is recommended that student aides be given course credit or certificates of achievement to reward them for their services.

Most untrained support staff will need to be trained on the job. The steps in training are:

1. Using the district's job description and evaluation instrument for the particular position, prioritize the skills in order from greatest to least immediacy.
2. Determine the skills already mastered by observing performance.
3. Plan systematic training in the remaining skills, to be addressed one at a time.

Supervision of media professionals is the responsibility of the school administration. Supervision of support staff is the responsibility of the head library media specialist (if that position is administrative) or of a school administrator with input from the media specialist. Periodic oral evaluations and annual written evaluations, using an appropriate instrument, should be conducted for each media staff member. These evaluations should result in suggestions for training or personal development.

COMPETENCY 0018 UNDERSTAND THE DEVELOPMENT, IMPLEMENTATION AND ONGOING EVALUATION OF A LIBRARY MEDIA PROGRAM

Skill 18.1 Using a needs assessment to establish program goals and to identify appropriate activities and resources to meet those goals

It is important to note that evaluation is an ongoing process. It must occur prior to determining goals and objectives and on a regular basis thereafter to ensure they are being met.

A wide variety of evaluation criteria may be used. The criteria include:

1. **Diagnostic standards** are based on conditions existing in programs that have already been judged excellent.
2. **Projective standards** are guidelines for ideal conditions.
3. **Quantitative standards** require numerical measurement.
4. **Qualitative standards** are based on observations, surveys, and interviews, without numerical measurements.

Most evaluations of school library media programs have been diagnostic or qualitative. Diagnostic prescriptions alone make no allowances for specific conditions in given schools and are often interpreted too literally; qualitative prescriptions alone are difficult to measure or sustain. Projective standards are usually broad national guidelines that serve best as long-range goals. Preferably, a program evaluation using both quantitative and qualitative standards produces results that can lead to modified objectives.

Statistics to substantiate progress toward quantitative goals can be derived from:

1. **Usage statistics** from automated circulation systems indicate frequency of use of materials.
2. **Inventory figures**, such as data on resource turnover, loss and damage, and missing materials indicate extent of use and replacement needs. Total materials count can substantiate compliance with criteria for materials per student.
3. **Individual circulation logs** indicate the frequency of patrons' use of library materials and the types of materials used.
4. **Class scheduling logs** indicate the proportion of staff and student body using materials and services, the frequency of use of specific resources or services, the age levels of users; specific subgroups served, and subject matter preferences, depending on the nature of data collected for scheduling.

Evidence of meeting qualitative standards can be derived from:

1. **Lesson plans** indicating the frequency of use of resources and specific classroom objectives planned cooperatively with faculty. Plans should also specify the effectiveness with which the students achieved the lesson objectives.
2. **Personnel evaluations.** Most districts make formative or summative evaluations of the professional, paraprofessional, and non-professional staff. Student aides should receive educational credit for their services hours. Their acquisition of specific skills and their final grades provide both quantitative and qualitative data.
3. **Surveys.** A systematic written evaluation should be conducted annually to obtain input from students, teachers, and parents on the success of program objectives.
4. **Conferences and Library Advisory Committee meetings.** Comments by faculty and students provide qualitative assessment of the value of the materials and services provided.
5. **Criterion-referenced or teacher-created tests** can be used to evaluate students' effectiveness in acquiring information skills or content area skills.

Skill 18.2 Recognize ways of involving the learning community in the formulation and communication of a long-range plan for the library media program (e.g., establishing a school library media planning team)

Once an initial program evaluation has been completed, program goals and objectives may be determined. These goals and objectives help to break down the overall vision into areas that the school feels are most important for the successful operation of a school library media program. Some of these goals may already be determined by national or state guidelines that district administrators have agreed to maintain. Some districts operate without a program to guide school library media centers. In that case, each school is responsible not only for setting its own criteria, but also for inspiring planning on the district level.

The first step is to define major goals. A goal is a broad statement of an intended outcome that reflects the mission of the school library media program that provides direction.

A goal is long-range. Therefore, when planning a school library media program based on an assessment of school and student characteristics, the program planning team should factor in these elements.

> **Learn more about creating long-range plans**
> http://www.libraryhq.com/plans.html

A long-range plan should:

1. Extend from 3 to 5 years.
2. Incorporate the goals of the other departments (grade levels or content teams) in the school.
3. Be stated in realistic terms. The goal should be an achievable aim, not a pipe dream.

Specific goals for school library media centers are outlined in *Information Power: Building Partnerships for Learning*. Key points include:

1. Providing access to resources and information through integrated activities on a variety of levels.
2. Providing physical access to a wide variety of resources and information from various locations including outside agencies and electronic resources.
3. Assisting patrons in locating and evaluating information.
4. Collaborating with teachers and others.
5. Facilitating the lifelong learning process.
6. Building a school library media program that acts as the hub of all learning within the school.
7. Providing resources that embrace cultural and social differences and support intellectual freedom.

After the major goals have been defined, objectives must be determined. An objective is a specific statement of a measurable result that will occur by a particular time, i.e. it must specify the conditions and criteria to be met effectively. Objectives reflect short-term priorities. Objectives have a specific format. They must contain an action verb and must be measurable. A few of the action verbs often seen in objectives are as follows: discuss, define, compare, identify, explain, and design.

An objective is to be achieved by means of a short-range plan. A short-range plan should be one part of a longer-range plan that is:

1. Accomplishable in one year or less.
2. Linked meaningfully in a logical progression to the expressed goal.
3. Flexible, as most objectives must be processed through affected groups before finalization.

In an Olympic year an appropriate example of goals and objectives might be:

Goal: To win an Olympic medal.

Objectives:

1. To increase my speed by 0.05 seconds per meter by June 30.
2. To double my practice time during the two weeks before the competition begins.
3. To lose 3 pounds before my weigh-in.

If translated into goals and objectives for library media centers it may read as follows:

Goal: To develop a collection more suited to the academic demands of the curriculum.

Objectives:

1. To increase the nonfiction collection by 10% in the next school year.
2. To ensure readability levels suited to gifted students for 5% of new selections.

Goal: To provide telecommunications services within three years.

Objectives:

1. To design a model for instructional use in 2005.
2. To plan for equipment and facilities needs in 2006.
3. To implement the model with a control group in 2007.

If a school seeks or wishes to maintain accreditation with the Middle States Association of Colleges and Schools, that organization's standards are an excellent source of program goals and objectives.

Skill 18.3 Applying procedures for evaluating the effectiveness of a library media program (e.g., with regard to collection, facility, personnel, etc.)

The purpose of evaluation is to determine whether all aspects of planning and implementation have been successfully accomplished. If evaluation shows unsuccessful outcomes, then the program must be modified. Successful outcomes can be used to confirm program objectives and to promote the media center programs.

Strategies for the use of program evaluation include:

1. Producing an annual report to be included in the school's annual report to parents or other publications for circulation in the community.
2. Review and modification of long-range goals and planning immediate changes in short-range goals.
3. Lobbying for budgetary or personnel support.
4. Soliciting assistance from faculty and administration in making curricular or instructional changes to maximize use of media center materials, equipment, and services.
5. Promoting **greater involvement of students** in academic and personal use of media center materials and services.

There are now so many outstanding resources, and the technology to easily identify them, that the task can be managed by following a few simple steps.

1. Rely on the information provided in this guide's resource list. If your school or district professional library does not contain these resources, use the resources of larger libraries in person or through interlibrary loan.
2. Give your school media program a close examination before doing your research. Study any written evaluations by media personnel, school improvement committees, library advisory committees, or annual reports. Informally survey a cross-section of students and teachers to gather input about their perceptions of the materials and services provided.
3. Make a list of questions based on the concerns that result from your evaluation. Peruse the questions in Chapter 1 of Information Power to see if there are any pertinent areas that have not yet been addressed.
4. Do your research.
5. Produce a written evaluation of your school's library media program based on your findings. Submit this evaluation to the principal and plan with her the best way to communicate the information to students, teachers, and parents.
6. Gather input from all groups to whom your evaluation is presented.
7. Meet with the Library Media Advisory Committee or equivalent group to formulate program changes. Be sure to include students and parents or lay community members on this committee.
8. Implement the changes and plan subsequent evaluations.

Sample Test

DIRECTIONS: Read each item and select the best response.

1. A school library media center should be an inviting space that encourages learning. To accomplish this, the school library media specialist should do all of the following except: *(Skill 1.1) Average Rigor*

    A. collaborate with school staff and students.
    B. create a schedule where each class comes to the media center each week for instruction.
    C. arrange materials so that they are easy to locate.
    D. promote the program as a wonderful place for learning.

2. Collaboration between the media specialist and classroom teacher is the key to an effective library media program. Which of the following scenarios best describes a media specialist willing to foster a collaborative partnership with a teacher? *(Skill 1.2) Rigorous*

    A. The media specialist meets only when approached by a classroom teacher who is asking for help.
    B. The media specialist can only meet on Tuesdays and Thursdays from 1-2 due to the fixed schedule that has been set up for the media center.
    C. The media specialist touches base with teachers on a regular basis and attends grade level planning sessions.
    D. The media specialist only meets with teachers on each grade level who are interested in working collaboratively.

3. To foster the collaborative process the media specialist must possess all of the following skills except: *(Skill 1.3) Easy*

    A. leadership
    B. flexibility
    C. perversity
    D. persistence

4. A school library media specialist is searching for ways to make the school library more effective. Which of the following would not be a successful strategy?
(Skill 1.4) Rigorous

   A. The school library media specialist develops activities that help to develop creativity and support critical thinking skills.
   B. The school library media specialist works in isolation to plan effective programs that support curriculum guidelines.
   C. The school library media specialist develops activities to expand students' interests and promote lifelong learning.
   D. The school library media specialist provides physical access to resources.

5. The media specialist is interested in beginning collaborative planning sessions with the teachers in the school, but not all of the teachers are interested. The media specialist should:
(Skill 1.3) Average rigor

   A. wait until all of the teachers are interested
   B. have the principal make all teacher collaboratively plan with the media specialist
   C. work with the teachers who are most willing to engage in the process
   D. abandon the idea

6. All of the following formats are best for small group learning except:
(Skill 3.4) Average rigor

   A. manipulatives
   B. computer projection
   C. photographs
   D. computer software

7. A statement defining the core principles of a school library media program is called the:
(Skill 1.5) Average rigor

   A. mission
   B. policy
   C. procedure
   D. objective

8. The media specialist needs to expand the collection to include a wider variety of resources for visually impaired students. Which of the following would be least beneficial?
   (Skill 1.6) Average Rigor

   A. Books with larger print.
   B. Books in Braille format.
   C. Books in audio format.
   D. Books in video format

9. Key design elements to consider when renovating or building a new facility include:
   (Skill 2.1) Average rigor

   A. Traffic flow
   B. Access for physically impaired users
   C. Security needs
   D. all of the above

10. A network allows which of the following to occur?
    (Skill 2.2) Average rigor

    A. sharing files.
    B. sharing printers.
    C. sharing software.
    D. all of the above

11. In a school with one full-time library media assistant (clerk), which of the following are responsibilities of the assistant?
    (Skill 2.3) Average rigor

    A. Selecting and ordering titles for the print collection.
    B. Performing circulation tasks and processing new materials.
    C. Providing in-servicing training to teachers on the integration of media materials into the school curriculum.
    D. Planning and implementing programs to involve parents and community.

12. Which of the following tasks should NOT be assigned to a volunteer?
    (Skill 2.3) Average rigor

    A. Decorating bulletin boards.
    B. Demonstrating use of retrieval systems.
    C. Maintaining bookkeeping records.
    D. Fundraising.

13. AASL/AECT guidelines recommend that student library aides be
(Skill 2.3) Average rigor

	A.	rewarded with grades or certificates for their service.
	B.	allowed to assist only during free time.
	C.	allowed to perform paraprofessional duties.
	D.	assigned tasks that relate to maintaining the atmosphere of the media center.

14. The most efficient method of evaluating support staff is to
(Skill 2.3) Average rigor

	A.	administer a written test.
	B.	survey faculty whom they serve.
	C.	observe their performance.
	D.	obtain verbal confirmation during an employee interview.

15. According to *Information Power*, which of the following is NOT a responsibility of the school library media specialist?
(Skill 2.3) Rigorous

	A.	maintaining and repairing equipment.
	B.	instructing educators and parents in the use of library media resources.
	C.	providing efficient retrieval systems for materials and equipment.
	D.	planning and implementing the library media center budget.

16. Collaborative partnerships with staff can take on many forms. All of the following are examples except:
(Skill 2.4) Rigorous

	A.	serving on curriculum development committees
	B.	viewing the school's curriculum and creating lessons
	C.	assisting teachers in planning, designing, and teaching lessons
	D.	assisting teachers and students with the use of new technologies

17. Collection development policies are developed to accomplish all of the following except
(Skill 2.5) Rigorous

	A.	guaranteeing users freedom to access information.
	B.	recognizing the needs and interests of users.
	C.	coordinating selection criteria and budget concerns.
	D.	recognizing rights of individuals or groups to challenge these policies.

18. The school library media center should be an inviting space that encourages learning. To accomplish this the school library media specialist should do all of the following except:
(Skill 2.6) Average rigor

   A. collaborate with school staff and students.
   B. create a schedule where each class comes to the media center each week for instruction.
   C. arrange materials so that they are easy to locate.
   D. promote the program as a wonderful place for learning.

19. The English I (9th Grade) teacher wants his students to become familiar with the contents of books in the reference area of the school library media center. He asks the library media specialist to recommend an activity to accomplish this goal. Which of the following activities would best achieve the goal?
(Skill 3.1) Average Rigor

   A. Assign a research paper on a specific social issues topic.
   B. Require a biography of a famous person.
   C. Design a set of questions covering a variety of topics and initiate a scavenger hunt approach to their location.
   D. Teach students the Dewey Decimal system and have them list several books in each Dewey subcategory.

20. A general statement or outcome that is broken down into specific skills. This statement is known as a:
(Skill 3.1) Average rigor

   A. policy
   B. procedure
   C. goal
   D. objective

21. The role of the library media specialist as a member of the school's curriculum team includes all of the following except
    (Skill 3.3) Rigorous

    A. ensuring a systematic approach to integrating information skills instruction.
    B. advising staff on appropriate learning styles to meet specific objectives.
    C. advising staff of current trends in curriculum design.
    D. advising staff of objectives design for specific content areas.

22. Which of the following formats is best for large group presentations?
    (Skill 3.4) Easy

    A. manipulatives
    B. multimedia
    C. audio recordings
    D. photographs

23. An elementary teacher, planning a unit on the local environment, finds materials that are too global or above her students' ability level. The best solution to this problem is to
    (Skill 3.5) Rigorous

    A. broaden the scope of the study to emphasize global concerns.
    B. eliminate the unit from the content.
    C. replace the unit with another unit that teaches the same skills.
    D. have the students design their own study materials using media production techniques.

24. The greatest benefit of learning media production techniques is that it helps
    (Skill 3.5) Rigorous

    A. the school reduce the need to purchase commercial products.
    B. the producer clarify his learning objectives.
    C. the teacher individualize instruction.
    D. the school library media specialist integrate information skills.

25. In the production of a teacher/student made audio-visual material, which of the following is NOT a factor in the planning phase?
(Skill 3.5) Rigorous

   A. stating the objectives.
   B. analyzing the audience.
   C. determining the purpose.
   D. selecting the format.

26. The first step for students designing their own videotape product is
(Skill 3.5) Average Rigor

   A. preparing the staging of indoor scenes.
   B. assembling a cast.
   C. creating a storyboard.
   D. calculating a budget.

27. Which of the following is determined first in deciding a media production format?
(Skill 3.5) Rigor

   A. the size and style of the artwork.
   B. the production equipment.
   C. the production materials.
   D. the method of display.

28. In assessing learning styles for staff development, consider that adults
(Skill 3.6) Rigorous

   A. are less affected by the learning environment than children.
   B. are more receptive to performing in and in front of groups.
   C. learn better when external motivations are guaranteed.
   D. demand little feedback.

29. Staff development activities in the use of materials and equipment are most effective if they
(Skills 3.6) Average Rigor

   A. are conducted individually as need is expressed.
   B. are sequenced in difficulty of operation or use.
   C. result in use of the acquired skills in classroom lessons.
   D. are evaluated for effectiveness.

30. Staff development is most effective when it includes:
(Skill 3.6) Average rigor

   A. continuing support
   B. hand-outs
   C. video tutorials
   D. stated objectives

31. Which of the following is the most desirable learning outcome of a staff development workshop on *Teaching with Interactive DVDS?* Participants
(Skill 3.6) Average Rigor

   A. score 80% or better on a post-test.
   B. design content specific lessons from multiple resources.
   C. sign up to take additional workshops.
   D. encourage other teachers to participate in future workshops.

32. According to AASL/AECT guidelines, in her role as *instructional consultant,* the school library media specialist uses her expertise to
(Skill 4.1) Average Rigor

   A. assist teachers in acquiring information skills which they can incorporate into classroom instruction.
   B. provide access to resource sharing systems.
   C. plan lessons in media production.
   D. provide staff development activities in equipment use.

33. Freedom of access of information for children includes all of the following except
(Skill 4.2) Average Rigor

   A. development of critical thinking.
   B. reflection of social growth.
   C. provision for religious differences.
   D. discrimination of different points of view.

34. AECT's Code of Ethics contains which of the following sections?
(Skill 4.2) Average Rigor

   A. Commitment to Media
   B. Commitment to Education
   C. Commitment to Society
   D. Commitment to School

35. A student looks for a specific title on domestic violence. When he learns it is overdue, he asks the library media specialist to tell him the borrower's name. The library media specialist should first
(Skill 4.3) Rigorous

   A. readily reveal the borrower's name.
   B. suggest he look for the book in another library.
   C. offer to put the boy's name on reserve pending the book's return.
   D. offer to request an interlibrary loan.

36. The Right to Read Statement was issued by:
    (Skill 4.4) Rigorous

    A. AECT
    B. ALA
    C. NCTE
    D. NICEM

37. In the landmark U.S. Supreme Court ruling in favor of Pico, the court's opinion established that
    (Skill 4.5) Rigorous

    A. library books, being optional not required reading, could not be arbitrarily removed by school boards.
    B. school boards have the same jurisdiction over library books as they have over textbooks.
    C. the intent to remove pervasively vulgar material is the same as the intent to deny free access to ideas.
    D. First Amendment challenges in regards to library books are the responsibility of appeals courts.

38. All of the following are benefits of interlibrary loan except:
    (Skill 5.2) Rigorous

    A. maximizing the use media center funds.
    B. providing a wider range of resources available for patrons.
    C. building partnerships with outside agencies.
    D. eliminating the need for media assistants.

39. A catalog that contains materials from several library collections is known as a
    (Skill 5.4) Easy

    A. Shared Catalog.
    B. Cooperative Catalog.
    C. Union Catalog.
    D. Universal Catalog

40. All of the following should be housed in the reference collection except:
    (Skill 6.1) Easy

    A. an atlas
    B. a dictionary
    C. a picture book
    D. a collection of encyclopedias

41. Which of the following media should be included in the school library media center's resource collection?
    (Skill 6.2) Rigorous

    A. audio recordings
    B. periodicals
    C. online resources
    D. all of the above

42. When selecting computer information databases for library media center computers, which of the following is the least important consideration?
    (Skill 6.3) Average rigor

    A. cost.
    B. format.
    C. user friendliness.
    D. ability levels of users

43. Which writer composes young adult literature in the fantasy genre?
    (Skill 7.1) Rigorous

    A. Stephen King.
    B. Piers Anthony.
    C. Virginia Hamilton.
    D. Phyllis Whitney.

44. Which fiction genre do these authors- Isaac Asimov, Louise Lawrence, and Andre Norton represent?
    (Skill 7.1) Rigorous

    A. adventure.
    B. romance.
    C. science fiction.
    D. fantasy.

45. All of the following are authors of fantasy except:
    (Skill 7.1) Rigorous

    A. Ray Bradbury
    B. Ursula LeGuin.
    C. Piers Anthony.
    D. Ann McCaffrey

46. All of the following are authors of young adult fiction EXCEPT
    (Skill 7.2) Rigorous

    A. Paul Zindel.
    B. Norma Fox Mazer.
    C. S.E. Hinton.
    D. Maurice Sendak.

47. When selecting books for students in grades k-2, it is best to choose books with which of the following characteristics?
    (Skill 7.3) Easy

    A. strong picture support
    B. familiar language patterns
    C. utilize cuing systems
    D. all of the above

48. The Caldecott Book Award was given to which book in 2002?
    (Skill 7.4) Rigorous

    A. *The Three Pigs* by David Wiesner
    B. *Had a Little Overcoat* Simms Taback
    C. *Golem* by David Wisniewski
    D. *Officer Buckle and Gloria* by Peggy Rathmann

49. Literature appreciation activities can include which of the following:
    (Skill 7.5) Easy

    A. author studies
    B. genre studies
    C. book talks
    D. all of the above

50. *The Horn Book* is
    (Skill 7.6) Average rigor

    A. a book about trumpets
    B. a children's picture book
    C. a professional journal
    D. a source for resource reviews

51. Which of the following is NOT one of three general criteria for selection of all materials?
    (Skill 8.2) Average Rigor

    A. authenticity.
    B. appeal.
    C. appropriateness.
    D. allocation.

52. Which of the following is a book jobber often used by school libraries:
    (Skill 8.2) Rigorous

    A. Library Media Book Services
    B. Baker and Taylor
    C. Mead and Blackwell
    D. Elementary Book Services

53. When a new media specialists comes to a library, it is important for them to be come familiar with the existing resource collection. One of the best ways to do this is to:
    (Skill 8.2) Average Rigor

    A. consult the district director regarding collection policies.
    B. browse the shelves to evaluate what is available.
    C. examine collections of other comparable schools.
    D. study the school's curriculum to understand the needs of users.

54. The role of the Media Committee or Media Advisory Committee is to assist with all of the following except:
    (Skill 8.3) Average rigor

    A. determine program direction
    B. evaluate the media specialist
    C. direct budget decisions
    D. collaborate with the media specialist

55. The process of discarding worn or outdated books and materials is known as:
    (Skill 8.4) Easy

    A. weeding
    B. inventory
    C. collection mapping
    D. eliminating

56. The practice of examining the quantity and quality of the school library media resource collection which provides a "snapshot" of the collection is called:
    (Skill 8.4) Easy

    A. collection development
    B. collection maintenance
    C. collection mapping
    D. weeding

57. Which of these Dewey Decimal classifications should be weeded most often?
    (Skill 8.4) Rigorous

    A. 100s
    B. 500s
    C. 700s
    D. Biographies

58. Which periodical contains book reviews of currently published children and young adult books?
(Skill 8.5) Rigorous

    A. Phi Delta Kappan
    B. School Library Journal
    C. School Library Media Quarterly
    D. American Teacher

59. To obtain a clear picture of the library media collection the media specialist can:
(Skill 8.6) Easy

    A. Read through the card catalog
    B. conduct a collection analysis
    C. ask teachers for their opinions
    D. none of the above

60. When selecting books for students in grades k-2, it is best to choose books with which of the following characteristics?
(Skill 9.1) Easy

    A. strong picture support
    B. familiar language patterns
    C. utilize cuing systems
    D. all of the above

61. The creators of the Big 6 Model are:
(Skill 9.2) Average Rigor

    A. Eisenberg and Berkowitz.
    B. Marzano and Bloom.
    C. Bloom and Gardner.
    D. Lance and Eisenberg.

62. Steps in the Big6 Model include all of the following except:
(Skill 9.2) Rigorous

    A. information seeking strategies
    B. location and access
    C. creation of information
    D. task definition

63. Skills that provide students with the ability to solve problems are known as
(Skill 9.3) Average rigor

    A. critical thinking skills
    B. multiple intelligences
    C. Loertscher's Taxonomies
    D. authentic learning

64. Students with disabilities would benefit from specialized software that can read online text, PDF documents and scanned pages. One popular software title is called:
(Skill 9.4) Rigorous

    A. Kurzweil Reader
    B. Accelerated Reader
    C. Star Reader
    D. Kertfeld Reader

65. The TAXONOMIES OF THE SCHOOL LIBRARY MEDIA PROGRAM outlines eleven levels of school library media specialists' involvement with curriculum and instruction and was developed by:
(Skill 9.5) Rigorous

    A. Eisenberg.
    B. Bloom.
    C. Loertscher.
    D. Lance.

66. All of the following organizations serve school libraries except:
    (Skill 9.6) Average Rigor

    A. AASL
    B. AECT
    C. ALCT
    D. ALA

67. Which of the following is true about essential questions?
    (Skill 10.1) Easy

    A. They are created by teachers to ensure they focus on curricular requirements.
    B. They are at the top of the Loertscher's Taxonomies.
    C. They are open-ended and focus on a broad topic.
    D. They should influence student thought.

68. When evaluating resources for effectiveness it is important to consider all of the following except:
    (Skill 10.2) Average Rigor

    A. style of the web page.
    B. the intended audience.
    C. whether or not the site is from a scholarly source.
    D. the scope of the information

69. A periodical index search which allows the user to pair Keywords with and, but, or or is called
    (Skill 10.3) Average Rigor

    A. Boolean.
    B. dialoguing.
    C. wildcarding.
    D. truncation.

70. A request from a social studies teacher for the creation of a list of historical fiction titles for a book report assignment is a _____ request.
    (Skill 10.4) Average Rigor

    A. ready reference.
    B. research.
    C. specific needs.
    D. complex search.

71. A search that uses specific terms to locate information is called a:
    (Skill 11.1) Average rigor

    A. reference search
    B. keyword search
    C. ready reference search
    D. operator search

72. A catalog that contains materials from several library collections is known as a
    (Skill 11.2) Average rigor

    A. Shared Catalog.
    B. Cooperative Catalog.
    C. Union Catalog.
    D. Universal Catalog.

73. Which of the following searches would most likely return the most results?
    (Skill 11.3) Average Rigor

    A. lions and tigers
    B. lions not tigers
    C. lions or tigers
    D. lions and not tigers

74. The media specialist is searching a database and needs to locate all of the entries that begin with the letter "P". What is the best way to format this search?
    (Skill *11.4) Average rigor*

    A. Create a search using the Boolean operator AND NOT. (P AND NOT A, B, C, D, E...)
    B. Place quotations around the letter P
    C. Use a wildcard
    D. This type of search cannot be done.

75. A keyword search returns too many results with few relevant records. What does the patron need to do?
    (Skill *12.2) Easy*

    A. narrow the search topic
    B. broaden the search topic
    C. find a new topic
    D. none of the above

76. A group of students in the business club will be creating a website to sell their product. When selecting their domain name, which of the following extensions would be best to use?
    (Skill 12.3) Rigorous

    A. .com
    B. .edu
    C. .cfm
    D. .html

77. A kindergarten class has just viewed a video on alligators. The best way to evaluate the suitability of the material for this age group is to
    (Skill 12.4) Rigorous

    A. test the students' ability to recall the main points of the video.
    B. compare this product to other similar products on this content.
    C. observe the body language and verbal comments during the viewing.
    D. ask the children to comment on the quality of the video at the end of the viewing.

78. In most learning hierarchies, which of the following is the highest order critical thinking skill?
    (Skill 12.5) Average Rigor

    A. appreciation.
    B. inference.
    C. recall.
    D. comprehension.

79. After reading *The Pearl,* a tenth grader asks, "Why can't we start sentences with *and* like John Steinbeck?" This student is showing the ability to
(Skill 12.5) Rigorous

   A. appreciate.
   B. comprehend.
   C. infer.
   D. evaluate.

80. A scoring guide that is generally subject and contains specific criteria in which projects should be judged is known as a:
(Skill 12.6) Easy

   A. rubric
   B. outline
   C. criteria
   D. evaluation

81. All but which of the following criteria are used when determining fair use of copyrighted material for classroom use?
(Skill 13.1) Average rigor

   A. Brevity Test.
   B. Spontaneity Test.
   C. Time Test.
   D. Cumulative Effect Test.

82. Section 108 of the Copyright Act permits the copying of an entire book if three conditions are met. Which of the following is NOT one of those conditions?
(Skill 13.1) Rigorous

   A. The library intends to allow inter- library loan of the book.
   B. The library is an archival library.
   C. The copyright notice appears on all the copies.
   D. The library is a public library.

83. Under the copyright brevity test, an educator may reproduce without written permission
(Skill 13.1) Rigorous

   A. 10% of any prose or poetry work.
   B. 500 words from a 5000 word article.
   C. 240 words of a 2400 word story.
   D. no work over 2500 words.

84. Licensing has become a popular means of copyright protection in the area of
(Skill 13.1) Average Rigor

   A. duplicating books for interlibrary loan.
   B. use of software application on multiple machines.
   C. music copying.
   D. making transparency copies of books or workbooks that are too expensive to purchase.

85. "Fair Use" policy in videotaping off-air from commercial television requires
    (Skill 13.1) Rigorous

    A. show in 5 days, erase by the 20th day.
    B. show in 10 days, erase by the 30th day.
    C. show in 10 days, erase by the 45th day.
    D. no restrictions.

86. MLA style is a popular format for citing resources in a bibliography. MLA is the acronym for:
    (Skill 13.2) Rigorous

    A. Media Library Association
    B. Modern Library Association
    C. Modern Literary Association
    D. Modern Language Association

87. When creating instructional materials which of the following is not a part of the planning phase?
    (Skill 13.3) Rigorous

    A. determining the goal or objectives to be covered
    B. create the media
    C. analyze the audience
    D. determine the purpose

88. Which of the following formats is best for large group presentations?
    (Skill 13.4) Easy

    A. manipulatives
    B. multimedia
    C. audio recordings
    D. photographs

89. All of the following formats are best for small group learning except:
    (Skill 13.4) Average rigor

    A. manipulatives
    B. computer projection
    C. photographs
    D. computer software

90. An elementary teacher, planning a unit on the local environment, finds materials that are too global or above her students' ability level. The best solution to this problem is to
    (Skill 13.5) Average rigor

    A. broaden the scope of the study to emphasize global concerns.
    B. eliminate the unit from the content.
    C. replace the unit with another unit that teaches the same skills.
    D. have the students design their own study materials using media production techniques.

91. The most effective method of initiating closer contacts with and determining the needs of classroom teachers is to
(Skill 14.1) Average Rigor

    A. ask to be included on the agenda of periodic faculty meetings.
    B. present after school or weekend in-services in opening communication channels.
    C. request permission to be included in grade-level or content-area meetings.
    D. establish a library advisory committee with one representative from each grade level or content area.

92. This outlines the role of the school library media specialist and the programs they manage.
(Skill 14.2) Rigorous

    A. Taxonomies of Learning
    B. Code of Ethics
    C. @ Your Library
    D. Library Bill of Rights

93. Which of the following is not a benefit of forming partnerships within the community?
(Skill 14.3) Average rigor

    A. increased support for media program
    B. decline in media resources
    C. provide wide array of resources
    D. increase parental involvement

94. Which of the following is NOT an expert in child development?
(Skill 14.4) Rigorous

    A. Lawrence Kohlberg.
    B. James Naisbitt.
    C. Jean Piaget.
    D. Erik Erikson.

95. Contemporary library media design models should consider which of the following an optional need?
(Skill 15.1) Rigorous

    A. flexibility of space to allow for reading, viewing, and listening.
    B. space for large group activities such as district meetings, standardized testing, and lectures.
    C. traffic flow patterns for entrance and exit from the media center as well as easy movement within the center.
    D. adequate and easy to rearrange storage areas for the variety of media formats and packaging style of modern materials.

96. Key design elements to consider when renovating or building a new facility include:
(Skill 15.1) Average rigor

    A. Traffic flow
    B. Access for physically impaired users
    C. Security needs
    D. all of the above

97. When automating a library catalog it is important to consider which of the following prior to set up?
    (Skill 15.2) Average rigor

    A. technical requirements
    B. loan period
    C. patron limitations
    D. color of spine labels

98. *Information Power: Building Partnerships for Learning* recommends flexible scheduling for
    (Skill 15.3) Easy

    A. elementary school library media centers.
    B. middle school library media centers.
    C. secondary school library media centers.
    D. all school library media centers.

99. When creating a schedule for a school library media center the type of schedule that maximizes access to resources is a:
    (Skill 15.3) Easy

    A. fixed schedule
    B. open schedule
    C. partial fixed schedule
    D. flexible schedule

100. The procedures for conducting an inventory of the media collection include all of the following except:
     (Skill 15.4) Rigorous

     A. Determine the cost of the inventory.
     B. Determine when the inventory will be conducted.
     C. Determine who will conduct the inventory.
     D. Determine if each item matches the information in the holding records.

101. The Library Bill of Rights includes all of the following except:
     (Skill 15.5) Rigorous

     A. Information presented in a library should be selected based upon the age level of the students.
     B. Resources should include a representation of all ideas, concepts, and backgrounds
     C. Resources should not be excluded because of viewpoint.
     D. Censorship should be challenged.

102. In which bibliographic field should information concerning the format of an audio-visual material appear?
     (Skill 16.1) Rigor

     A. Material specific details.
     B. Physical description.
     C. Notes.
     D. Standard numbers.

LIBRARY & MEDIA SPECIALIST

103. MARC is the acronym for:
(Skill 16.1) Easy

    A.   Mobile Accessible Recorded Content
    B.   Machine Accessible Readable Content
    C.   Machine Readable Content
    D.   Mobile Accessible Readable Content

104. AACR2 is the acronym for:
(Skill 16.1) Easy

    A.   Anglo-American Cataloging Rules Second Edition
    B.   American Association of Cataloging Rules Second Edition
    C.   American Association of Content Rules Second Edition
    D.   Anglo-American Content Rules Second Edition

105. OCLC is the acronym for:
(Skill 16.1) Average rigor

    A.   Online Computer Library Center
    B.   Online Computer Library Catalog
    C.   Online Computer Library Conference
    D.   Online Computer Library Content

106. In MARC records the title information can be found under which tag?
(Skill 16.1) Rigorous

    A.   130
    B.   245
    C.   425
    D.   520

107. Collection development policies are developed to accomplish all of the following except
(Skill 16.3) Rigorous

    A.   guarantee users freedom to access information.
    B.   recognize the needs and interests of users.
    C.   coordinate selection criteria and budget concerns.
    D.   recognize rights of individuals or groups to challenge these policies.

108. All of the following are components of a circulation policy except:
(Skill 16.4) Rigorous

    A.   loan period
    B.   process for handling overdues
    C.   limitations
    D.   location to post borrower's name

109. Ongoing evaluation is necessary to produce a quality media program. Use of evaluation results be used for all of the following except:
(Skill 16.5) Easy

   A. lobbying for budgetary or personnel support
   B. to make changes to the use of the media center materials
   C. to determine circulation regulations
   D. all of the above

110. Which of the following are examples of ways to promote the school library media programs:
(Skill 17.2) Easy

   A. Attend school board meetings
   B. Serve on the school's curriculum committee
   C. Invite school board members to media planning meetings
   D. All of the above

111. In formulating an estimated collection budget consider all of the following except
(Skill 17.3) Rigorous

   A. attrition by loss, damage, or age.
   B. the maximum cost of item replacement.
   C. the number of students served.
   D. the need for expansion to meet minimum guidelines.

112. The most appropriate means of obtaining extra funds for library media programs is
(Skill 17.4) Average Rigor

   A. having candy sales.
   B. conducting book fairs.
   C. charging fines.
   D. soliciting donations.

113. A school with 500 – 749 students should have how many media specialists?
(Skill 17.5) Easy

   A. 1 part-time media specialist
   B. 1 full time media specialist
   C. 2 full time media specialist
   D. no media specialist required

114. The most efficient method of evaluating support staff is to
(Skill 17.6) Average rigor

   A. administer a written test.
   B. survey faculty whom they serve.
   C. observe their performance.
   D. obtain verbal confirmation during an employee interview.

115. Which of the following is an example of quantitative data that would be used to evaluate a school library media program?
(Skill 18.1) Average rigor

   A. Personnel evaluations
   B. Usage statistics
   C. Surveys
   D. Interviews

116. An accredited elementary school has maintained an acceptable number of items in its print collection for ten years. In the evaluation review, this fact is evidence of both
(Skill 18.1) Rigorous

    A. diagnostic and projective standards.
    B. diagnostic and quantitative standards.
    C. projective and quantitative standards.
    D. projective and qualitative standards.

117. The principal is completing the annual report. He needs to include substantive data on use of the media center. In addition to the number of book circulations, he would like to know the proportionate use of the media center's facilities and services by the various grade levels or content areas. This information can most quickly be obtained from:
(Skill 18.1) Rigorous

    A. the class scheduling log.
    B. student surveys.
    C. lesson plans.
    D. inventory figures

118. A general statement or outcome that is broken down into specific skills. This statement is known as a:
(Skill 18.2) Average rigor

    A. policy
    B. procedure
    C. goal
    D. objective

119. A statement defining the core principles of a school library media program is called the:
(Skill 18.2) Average rigor

    A. mission
    B. policy
    C. procedure
    D. objective

120. Which of the following is a library policy, not a procedure?
(Skill 18.2) Rigorous

    A. providing a vehicle for the circulation of audio-visual equipment.
    B. setting guidelines for collection development.
    C. determining the method for introducing an objective into the school improvement plan.
    D. setting categorical limits on operating expenses.

121. A procedure is:
(Skill 18.2) Easy

    A. a course of action taken to execute a plan.
    B. a written statement of principle used to guarantee a management practice.
    C. a statement of core values of an organization.
    D. a regulation concerning certification.

122. Long range plans should span how many years?
    (Skill 18.3) Easy

    A. 2 – 4
    B. 3 – 5
    C. 5 – 10
    D. 10 – 15

123. Ongoing evaluation is necessary to produce a quality media program. Use of evaluation results be used for all of the following except:
    (Skill 18.4) Rigorous

    A. lobbying for budgetary or personnel support
    B. to make changes to the use of the media center materials
    C. to determine circulation regulations
    D. all of the above

124. Parent involvement is critical to the support of a school and media program. Which of the following is the least effective way to increase parent involvement:
    (Skill 7.5) Easy

    A. Plan special family nights.
    B. Plan parent workshops
    C. Involve parents as volunteers.
    D. Send notes home to parents

125. For students to take responsibility for their own learning the media specialist much teach them all of the following but:
    (Skill 7.5) Easy

    A. locate resources.
    B. evaluate resources.
    C. purchase resources
    D. use resources.

TEACHER CERTIFICATION STUDY GUIDE

Answer Key

1.	B	33.	C	65.	C	97.	A
2.	B	34.	C	66.	C	98.	D
3.	C	35.	C	67.	C	99.	D
4.	B	36.	C	68.	A	100.	A
5.	C	37.	A	69.	A	101.	A
6.	D	38.	D	70.	C	102.	C
7.	A	39.	C	71.	B	103.	C
8.	D	40.	C	72.	C	104.	A
9.	D	41.	D	73.	C	105.	A
10.	D	42.	A	74.	C	106.	B
11.	B	43.	B	75.	A	107.	C
12.	C	44.	C	76.	A	108.	D
13.	A	45.	A	77.	C	109.	D
14.	C	46.	D	78.	A	110.	D
15.	A	47.	D	79.	D	111.	B
16.	B	48.	A	80.	A	112.	B
17.	C	49.	D	81.	C	113.	B
18.	B	50.	D	82.	A	114.	C
19.	C	51.	D	83.	B	115.	B
20.	C	52.	B	84.	B	116.	B
21.	D	53.	B	85.	C	117.	A
22.	B	54.	B	86.	D	118.	C
23.	D	55.	A	87.	B	119.	A
24.	B	56.	C	88.	B	120.	B
25.	D	57.	B	89.	D	121.	A
26.	C	58.	B	90.	C	122.	B
27.	D	59.	B	91.	C	123.	D
28.	B	60.	D	92.	C	124.	D
29.	C	61.	A	93.	B	125.	C
30.	A	62.	C	94.	B		
31.	B	63.	A	95.	B		
32.	D	64.	A	96.	D		

Rigor Table

Easy (25 questions, 20% of test)	Average Rigor (50 questions, 40% of test)	Rigorous (50 questions, 40% of test)
3, 22, 39, 40, 47, 49, 55, 56, 59, 60, 67, 75, 80, 88, 98, 99, 103, 104, 109, 110, 113, 121, 122, 124, 125	1, 5, 6, 7, 8, 9, 10, 11, 12, 13, 14, 8, 19, 20, 26, 29, 30, 31, 32, 33, 34, 42, 50, 51, 53, 54, 61, 63, 66, 68, 69, 71, 72, 73, 74, 78, 81, 84, 89, 90, 91, 93, 96, 97, 105, 112, 114, 115, 118, 119	2, 4, 15, 16, 17, 21, 23, 24, 25, 27, 28, 35, 36, 37, 38, 41, 43, 44, 45, 46, 48, 52, 57, 58, 62, 64, 65, 70, 76, 77, 79, 82, 83, 85, 86, 87, 92, 94, 95, 100, 101, 102, 106, 107, 108, 111, 116, 117, 120, 123

TEACHER CERTIFICATION STUDY GUIDE

Rationales with Sample Questions

1. The school library media center should be an inviting space that encourages learning. To accomplish this, the school library media specialist should do all of the following except:
   (Skill 1.1) Average Rigor

   A. collaborate with school staff and students.
   B. create a schedule where each class comes to the media center each week for instruction.
   C. arrange materials so that they are easy to locate.
   D. promote the program as a wonderful place for learning.

Answer: B. create a schedule where each class comes to the media center each week for instruction

The goal of a school library is to operate under a flexible schedule to maximize use of the media center and its resources. This makes Option B the most appropriate answer.

2. Collaboration between the media specialist and classroom teacher is the key to an effective library media program. Which of the following scenarios best describes a media specialist willing to foster a collaborative partnership with a teacher?
   (Skill 1.2) Rigorous

   A. The media specialist meets only when approached by a classroom teacher who is asking for help.
   B. The media specialist can only meet on Tuesdays and Thursdays from 1-2 due to the fixed schedule that has been set up for the media center.
   C. The media specialist touches base with teachers on a regular basis and attends grade level planning sessions.
   D. The media specialist only meets with teachers on each grade level who are interested in working collaboratively.

Answer: B. The media specialist can only meet on Tuesdays and Thursdays from 1-2 due to the fixed schedule that has been set up for the media center.

A flexible schedule is most conducive to fostering the collaborative process with teachers. When a media specialist is on a fixed schedule and only has a limited time each week to plan with teachers, the media specialist loses some of their effectiveness. Option B is the most appropriate answer.

3. **To foster the collaborative process the media specialist must possess all of the following skills except:**
   (Skill 1.3) Easy

   A. leadership
   B. flexibility
   C. be perverse
   D. persistence

Answer: C. Be perverse.

A school library media specialist must be flexible, possess good leadership skills, and be persistent making Option C the most appropriate response.

4. **A school library media specialist is searching for ways to make the school library more effective. Which of the following would not be a successful strategy?**
   (Skill 1.4) Rigorous

   A. The school library media specialist develops activities that help to develop creativity and support critical thinking skills.
   B. The school library media specialist works in isolation to plan effective programs that support curriculum guidelines.
   C. The school library media specialist develops activities to expand students' interests and promote lifelong learning.
   D. The school library media specialist provides physical access to resources.

Answer: B. The school library media specialist works in isolation to plan effective programs that support curriculum guidelines.

For a media program to be most effective, the media specialist should work closely with classroom teachers to form a strong collaborative partnership. While a media specialist may have to work in isolation to plan effective programs, it is not the most desired result. This makes Option B the most appropriate answer.

5. The media specialist is interested in beginning collaborative planning sessions with the teachers within the school, but not all of the teachers are interested. The media specialist should:
   (Skill 1.3) Average rigor

   A. wait until all of the teachers are interested
   B. have the principal make all teachers collaboratively plan with the media specialist
   C. work with the teachers who are most willing to engage in the process
   D. abandon the idea

Answer: C. work with the teachers who are most willing to engage in the process

A good place for media specialists to begin forming collaborative relationships is with those who are willing. As the media specialist gains confidence and support they need to branch out to meet with all teachers. Planning with teachers during grade level meetings is an ideal way to enhance the process.

6. All of the following formats are best for small group learning except:
   (Skill 3.4) Average rigor

   A. manipulatives
   B. computer projection
   C. photographs
   D. computer software

Answer: D. computer software

Computer software used on a single machine is most appropriate for small groups. The most appropriate answer is Option D.

7. A statement defining the core principles of a school library media program is called the:
   (Skill 1.5) Average Rigor

   A. mission
   B. policy
   C. procedure
   D. objective

Answer: A. mission

The core principles of an organization are outlined in a mission statement. An objective is a specific statement of measurable result that reflects the mission statement.

8. The media specialist needs to expand the collection to include a wider variety of resources for visually impaired students. Which of the following would be least beneficial?
   (Skill 3.8) Average Rigor

   A. Books with larger print.
   B. Books in Braille format.
   C. Books in audio format.
   D. Books in video format.

Answer: D. Books in video format.

Books in video format would be least beneficial. Students with visual impairments would have a more difficult time gaining information from this format than any of the other formats listed.

9. Key design elements to consider when renovating or building a new facility include:
   (Skill 2.1) Average rigor

   A. Traffic flow
   B. Access for physically impaired users
   C. Security needs
   D. all of the above

Answer: D. all of the above

Whether planning for a new media center or renovating an existing one there are many things that need to be taken into consideration. Among the considerations are the traffic flow, plans for access for impaired users and security. Other considerations would be appropriate space for specific tasks and furniture height. This makes Option D the most appropriate answer.

10. A network allow which of the following to occur?
    (Skill 2.2) Average rigor

    A. sharing files.
    B. sharing printers.
    C. sharing software.
    D. all of the above

Answer: D. all of the above.

A network allows the sharing of files, printers, and software. This makes Option D the most appropriate response.

11. In a school with one full-time library media assistant (clerk), which of the following are responsibilities of the assistant?
    (Skill 2.3) Average Rigor

    A. selecting and ordering titles for the print collection.
    B. performing circulation tasks and processing new materials.
    C. inservicing teachers on the integration of media materials into the school curriculum.
    D. planning and implementing programs to involve parents and community.

Answer: B. performing circulation tasks and processing new materials.

Option B is the most appropriate answer. Circulation tasks and the processing of materials generally involve clerical duties. The other options are usually performed by a licensed media specialists.

12. Which of the following tasks should a volunteer NOT be asked to perform?
    (Skill 2.3) Average Rigor

    A. decorating bulletin boards.
    B. demonstrating use of retrieval systems.
    C. maintaining bookkeeping records.
    D. fundraising.

Answer: C. maintaining bookkeeping records.

Volunteers are crucial to the effective running of a school library media center. Their assistance is invaluable in the areas of clerical tasks, creative tasks, or promoting the media center. However, the media specialist should be responsible for maintaining bookkeeping records to ensure the budgets are managed well, making Option C the most appropriate answer.

13. **AASL/AECT guidelines recommend that student library aides be (Skill 2.3) Average Rigor**

    A. rewarded with grades or certificates for their service.
    B. allowed to assist only during free time.
    C. allowed to perform paraprofessional duties.
    D. assigned tasks that relate to maintaining the atmosphere of the media center.

Answer: A. rewarded with grades or certificates for their service.

It is important to recognize students for the valuable service they perform as student library aides. In younger grades that recognition can come in the form or certificates. High school or middle school students may be a library aide as part of their course requirements. In this case, outstanding performance would be recognized in the form of grades. Option A is the most appropriate answer.

14. **The most efficient method of evaluating support staff is to (Skill 2.3) Average Rigor**

    A. administer a written test.
    B. survey faculty whom they serve.
    C. observe their performance.
    D. obtain verbal confirmation during an employee interview.

Answer: C. observe their performance

The most efficient method of evaluating support staff is to observe their performance. An observation can provide an overall picture of the tasks they routinely perform. Observations may be conducted by the media specialist alone or in conjunction with another school administrator or fellow media specialist.

TEACHER CERTIFICATION STUDY GUIDE

15. According to *Information Power*, which of the following is NOT a responsibility of the school library media specialist?
    (Skill 2.3) Rigorous

    A. maintaining and repairing equipment.
    B. instructing educators and parents in the use of library media resources.
    C. providing efficient retrieval systems for materials and equipment.
    D. planning and implementing the library media center budget.

Answer: A. maintaining and repairing equipment

While the school library media specialist is responsible for program administration and aiding with instruction, their responsibilities do not include maintaining and repairing equipment. This is generally the duty of an assistant or technician

16. Collaborative partnerships with staff can take on many forms. All of the following are examples except:
    (Skill 2.4) Rigorous

    A. serving on curriculum development committees
    B. viewing the school's curriculum and creating lessons
    C. assisting teachers in planning, designing, and teaching lessons
    D. assisting teachers and students with the use of new technologies

Answer: B. viewing the school's curriculum and creating lessons

For the collaborative process to be effective the media specialist needs to work closely with the classroom teacher to create and plan lessons. The planning should not be conducted by the media specialist alone. This may occur, but it is not the desired result. Option B is the most appropriate answer.

LIBRARY & MEDIA SPECIALIST

17. Collection development policies are developed to accomplish all of the following except
    (Skill 2.5) Rigorous

    A. guarantee users freedom to access information.
    B. recognize the needs and interests of users.
    C. coordinate selection criteria and budget concerns.
    D. recognize rights of individuals or groups to challenge these policies.

Answer: C. coordinate selection criteria and budget concerns

The main goal of a collection development policy is to set guidelines and procedures that govern how resources are purchased and managed. It does not coordinate any criteria or address funding issues.

18. The school library media center should be an inviting space that encourages learning. To accomplish this the school library media specialist should do all of the following except:
    (Skill 2.6) Average rigor

    A. collaborate with school staff and students.
    B. create a schedule where each class comes to the media center each eek for instruction.
    C. arrange materials so that they are easy to locate.
    D. promote the program as a wonderful place for learning.

Answer: B. create a schedule where each class comes to the media center each week for instruction

The goal of a school library is to operate under a flexible schedule to maximize use of the media center and its resources. This makes Option B the most appropriate answer.

19. The English I (9th Grade) teacher wants his students to become familiar with the contents of books in the reference area of the school library media center. He asks the library media specialist to recommend an activity to accomplish this goal. Which of the following activities would best achieve the goal?
    (Skill 3.1) Average Rigor

    A. Assign a research paper on a specific social issues topic.
    B. Require a biography of a famous person.
    C. Design a set of questions covering a variety of topics and initiate a scavenger hunt approach to their location.
    D. Teach students the Dewey Decimal system and have them list several books in each Dewey subcategory.

Answer: C. Design a set of questions covering a variety of topics and initiate a scavenger hunt approach to their location.

Students often learn best by doing. If the teacher's goal was for students to learn to use reference materials, then the best way to accomplish this is to design a task that does just that. In this case the students are applying their knowledge making Option C the best answer.

20. A general statement or outcome that is broken down into specific skills. This statement is known as a:
    (Skill 3.1) Average rigor

    A. policy
    B. procedure
    C. goal
    D. objective

Answer: C. goal

A goal is a general statement or outcome that is broken down into specific measurable objectives. Option C is the most appropriate answer.

TEACHER CERTIFICATION STUDY GUIDE

21. As a member of the school's curriculum team, the library media specialist's role would include all of the following except
    (Skill 3.3) Rigorous

    A. ensuring a systematic approach to integrating information skills instruction.
    B. advising staff on appropriate learning styles to meet specific objectives.
    C. advising staff of current trends in curriculum design.
    D. advising staff of objectives designed for specific content areas.

Answer: D. advising staff of objectives designed for specific content areas.

The school library media specialist can lend their expertise in the area of information skills integration, learning styles, and current trends in curriculum design. It is best to let the content area teachers plan for their specific objectives and the media specialist serve as a support person as listed previously.

22. Which of the following formats is best for large group presentations?
    (Skill 3.4) Easy

    A. manipulatives
    B. multimedia
    C. audio recordings
    D. photographs

Answer: B. multimedia

Multimedia presentations are most appropriate for large groups. When used in conjunction with projectors and large screens, multimedia presentations are very effective.

23. **An elementary teacher, planning a unit on the local environment, finds materials that are too global or above her students' ability level. The best solution to this problem is to**
    (Skill 3.5) Rigorous

    A. broaden the scope of the study to emphasize global concerns.
    B. eliminate the unit from the content.
    C. replace the unit with another unit that teaches the same skills.
    D. have the students design their own study materials using media production techniques.

Answer: D. have the students design their own study materials using media production techniques.

When commercial materials cannot be found to meet student needs, the best alternative is to have students design their own materials. By designing and creating their own materials students tend to develop a deeper understanding of the material.

24. **The greatest benefit of learning media production techniques is that it helps**
    (Skill 3.5) Rigorous

    A. the school reduce the need to purchase commercial products.
    B. the producer clarify his learning objectives.
    C. the teacher individualize instruction.
    D. the school library media specialist integrate information skills.

Answer: B. the producer clarify his learning objectives.

The greatest benefit of media production generally comes to the producer. This is the person in charge of the production. To make the production most effective the producer must clarify his/her goals and specifically outline the learning objectives. This makes Option B the most appropriate answer.

TEACHER CERTIFICATION STUDY GUIDE

25. In the production of a teacher/student-made audio-visual material, which of the following is NOT a factor in the planning phase?
    (Skill 3.5) Rigorous

    A. stating the objectives.
    B. analyzing the audience.
    C. determining the purpose.
    D. selecting the format.

Answer: D. selecting the format.

In planning for any audio-visual materials, as in planning any student work, it is important to determine the purpose, analyze the audience, and state the objectives. While selecting the format is important, though it is not one of the first steps that must be taken.

26. The first step for students designing their own videotape product is
    (Skill 3.5) Average Rigor

    A. preparing the staging of indoor scenes.
    B. assembling a cast.
    C. creating a storyboard.
    D. calculating a budget.

Answer: C. creating a storyboard.

The correct answer is Option C. A storyboard is a series of panels that provide a rough sketch of each scene in a video.

27. Which of the following is determined first in deciding a media production format?
    (Skill 3.5) Rigor

    A. the size and style of the artwork.
    B. the production equipment.
    C. the production materials.
    D. the method of display.

Answer: D. the method of display.

How the media will be displayed will depend upon the format of the media. It will determine the size and style of the artwork and the equipment that would be used. It is Option D, the method of display that will determine the production format.

LIBRARY & MEDIA SPECIALIST

28. **In assessing learning styles for staff development, consider that adults**
    (Skill 3.6) Rigorous

    A. are less affected by the learning environment than children.
    B. are more receptive to performing in and in front of groups.
    C. learn better when external motivations are guaranteed.
    D. demand little feedback.

Answer: B. are more receptive to performing in front of groups.

Adult learners often need as much feedback on performance as their students would especially when learning new skills. They are affected by their learning environments and will still perform even if there are no external rewards. It is Option B that is the correct answer. Adult learners are more receptive to performing in front of groups.

29. **Staff development activities in the use of materials and equipment are most effective if they**
    (Skills 3.6) Average Rigor

    A. are conducted individually as need is expressed.
    B. are sequenced in difficulty of operation or use.
    C. result in use of the acquired skills in classroom lessons.
    D. are evaluated for effectiveness.

Answer: C. Result in use of the acquired skills in classroom lessons.

Option C is the most appropriate answer. The ultimate goal of most staff development activities is use or integration in the classroom.

30. **Staff development is most effective when it includes:**
    (Skill 3.6) Average rigor

    A. continuing support
    B. hand-outs
    C. video tutorials
    D. stated objectives

Answer: A. continuing support

While the other options are important to consider when providing staff development, it is the provision of continuing support that ensures the information learned will used to its fullest potential. Option A is the most appropriate answer.

TEACHER CERTIFICATION STUDY GUIDE

31. Which of the following is the most desirable learning outcome of a staff development workshop on *Teaching with Interactive DVDS*? Participants
    (Skill 3.6) Average Rigor

    A. score 80% or better on a post- test.
    B. design content specific lessons from multiple resources.
    C. sign up to take additional workshops.
    D. encourage other teachers to participate in future workshops.

Answer: B. Design content specific lessons from multiple resources.

The purpose of most staff development workshops is to foster integration of resources into the classroom. Performance and attendance in future workshops is desirable, but not the main goal.

32. According to AASL/AECT guidelines, in her role as *instructional consultant,* the school library media specialist uses her expertise to *(Skill 4.1) Average Rigor*

    A. assist teachers in acquiring information skills which they can incorporate into classroom instruction.
    B. provide access to resource sharing systems.
    C. plan lessons in media production.
    D. provide staff development activities in equipment use.

Answer: D. provide staff development activities in equipment use.

As an instructional consultant, the school library media specialist does provide staff development activities. Providing access is part of the role of program administrator. Assisting teachers and planning lessons is part of the teaching role of a media specialist. This makes Option D the most appropriate answer.

33. **Freedom of access of information for children includes all of the following except**
    (Skill 4.2) Average Rigor

    A. development of critical thinking.
    B. reflection of social growth.
    C. provision for religious differences.
    D. discrimination of different points of view.

Answer: C. Provision for religious differences.

The Freedom of Access of Information for children does not include provisions for religious differences making Option C the best answer. It does provide for freedom to form and express opinions.

34. **AECT's Code of Ethics contains which of the following sections?**
    (Skill 4.2) Average Rigor

    A. Commitment to Media
    B. Commitment to Education
    C. Commitment to Society
    D. Commitment to School

Answer: C. Commitment to Society.

There are four sections found in AECT's Code of Ethics: Preamble, Commitment to Individual, Commitment to Society, Commitment to Profession. This makes Option C the most appropriate answer.

TEACHER CERTIFICATION STUDY GUIDE

35. A student looks for a specific title on domestic violence. When he learns it is overdue, he asks the library media specialist to tell him the borrower's name. The library media specialist should first *(Skill 4.3) Rigorous*

    A. readily reveal the borrower's name.
    B. suggest he look for the book in another library.
    C. offer to put the boy's name on reserve pending the book's return.
    D. offer to request an interlibrary loan.

Answer: C. Offer to put the boy's name on reserve pending the book's return.

Patron confidentiality is of the utmost importance. The media specialist also needs to meet the needs of the patron requesting the book. The most appropriate course of action is Option C, offer to put the boy's name on reserve pending the book's return.

36. The Right to Read Statement was issued by:
    (Skill 4.4) Rigorous

    A. AECT
    B. ALA
    C. NCTE
    D. NICEM

Answer: C. NCTE.

The National Council of Teachers of English (NCTE) is responsible for the creation of the Right to Read Statement. This make Option C the most appropriate answer.

37. **In the landmark U.S. Supreme Court ruling in favor of Pico, the court's opinion established that**
    (Skill 4.5) Rigorous

    A. library books, being optional not required reading, could not be arbitrarily removed by school boards.
    B. school boards have the same jurisdiction over library books as they have over textbooks.
    C. the intent to remove pervasively vulgar material is the same as the intent to deny free access to ideas.
    D. First Amendment challenges in regards to library books are the responsibility of appeals courts.

Answer: A. Library books, being optional not required reading, could not be arbitrarily removed by school boards.

In the Supreme Court Case: Board of Education, Island Trees Union Free School District No. 26 v. Pico states that library books, being optional not required reading, could not be arbitrarily removed by school boards.

38. **All of the following are benefits of interlibrary loan except:**
    (Skill 5.2) Rigorous

    A. maximizing the use media center funds.
    B. providing a wider range of resources available for patrons.
    C. building partnerships with outside agencies.
    D. eliminating the need for media assistants.

Answer: D. eliminating the need for media assistants

The most appropriate response is Option D. Interlibrary loan allows the cooperating entities to maximize both funds and resources. It does not eliminate the need for media assistants.

TEACHER CERTIFICATION STUDY GUIDE

39. A catalog that contains materials from several library collections is known as a
    (Skill 5.4) Easy

    A. Shared Catalog.
    B. Cooperative Catalog.
    C. Union Catalog.
    D. Universal Catalog.

Answer: C. Union Catalog

Option C is the most appropriate answer. A union catalog exists when various entities combine their resource lists so that they can be shown in one catalog. This is most often done throughout school districts or through partnerships with colleges and universities.

40. All of the following should be housed in the reference collection except:
    (Skill 6.1) Easy

    A. an atlas
    B. a dictionary
    C. a picture book
    D. a collection of encyclopedias

Answer: C. a picture book

While a picture book that is part of a special collection may be housed in a reference collection, normal picture books are not a part of the reference collection. Option C is the most appropriate answer.

41. Which of the following media should be included in the school library media center's resource collection?
    (Skill 6.2) Rigorous

    A. audio recordings
    B. periodicals
    C. online resources
    D. all of the above

Answer: D. all of the above

A school library media collection should contain a wide array of materials in various formats. Audio recordings, periodicals, and online resources should be a par of the collection as well as many other types of resources. This makes Option D the most appropriate answer.

42. When selecting computer information databases for library media center computers, which of the following is the least important consideration?
    (Skill 6.3) Average Rigor

    A. cost.
    B. format.
    C. user friendliness.
    D. ability levels of users.

Answer: A. cost

When purchasing computer software it is most important to consider the end users. The software must be easy to use and meet the desired needs. Cost must be taken into consideration but it should not be the absolute determiner for purchasing software. Option A is the least important consideration.

TEACHER CERTIFICATION STUDY GUIDE

43. Which writer composes young adult literature in the fantasy genre?
    (Skill 7.1) Rigorous

    A. Stephen King.
    B. Piers Anthony.
    C. Virginia Hamilton.
    D. Phyllis Whitney.

Answer: B. Piers Anthony

Piers Anthony is the author of such books as *Ghost*, *Firefly*, and *Bio of an Ogre*. He is the only author listed that writes fantasy for young adults.

44. Which fiction genre do these authors- Isaac Asimov, Louise Lawrence, and Andre Norton represent?
    (Skill 7.1) Rigorous

    A. adventure.
    B. romance.
    C. science fiction.
    D. fantasy.

Answer: C. science fiction.

All of these authors represent Option C. Science fiction titles for each include:
Asimov- *I Robot, Foundation Trilogy*
Lawrence – *Children of the Dust, Moonwind*
Norton – *Stargate, Android at Arms*

45. All of the following are authors of fantasy except:
    (Skill 7.1) Rigorous

    A. Ray Bradbury
    B. Ursula LeGuin.
    C. Piers Anthony.
    D. Ann McCaffrey

Answer: A. Ray Bradbury

The most appropriate answer is Option A. Ray Bradbury is a science fiction author and the others are fantasy writers.

LIBRARY & MEDIA SPECIALIST

46. **All of the following are authors of young adult fiction EXCEPT**
    (Skill 7.2) Rigorous

    A. Paul Zindel.
    B. Norma Fox Mazer.
    C. S.E. Hinton.
    D. Maurice Sendak.

Answer: D. Maurice Sendak

Maurice Sendak is best know for his picture books for young children such as *Where the Wild Things Are*.

47. **When selecting books for students in grades k-2, it is best to choose books with which of the following characteristics?**
    (Skill 7.3) Easy

    A. strong picture support
    B. familiar language patterns
    C. utilize cuing systems
    D. all of the above

Answer: D. all of the above

The best answer is Option D. Young readers need books that have strong picture support, repetitive language patterns, and strong cuing systems.

48. **The Caldecott Book Award was given to which book in 2002?**
    (Skill 7.4) Rigorous

    A. *The Three Pigs* by David Wiesner
    B. *Had a Little Overcoat* Simms Taback
    C. *Golem* by David Wisniewski
    D. *Officer Buckle and Gloria* by Peggy Rathmann

Answer: A. *The Three Pigs* by David Wiesner

The correct answer is Option A. *Had a Little Overcoat* is the 2000 winner. *Golem* is the 1997 winner. *Officer Buckle and Gloria* is the 1996 winner.

49. Literature appreciation activities can include which of the following:
    (Skill 7.5) Easy

    A. author studies
    B. genre studies
    C. book talks
    D. all of the above

Answer: D. all of the above

Literature appreciation activities can include: author studies, book talks, genre studies, among other activities. That makes Option D the most appropriate answer.

50. *The Horn Book* is
    (Skill 7.6) Average Rigor

    A. a book about trumpets
    B. a children's picture book
    C. a professional journal
    D. a source for resource reviews

Answer: D. a source for resource review

The Horn Book is a collective review resource that lists book reviews as well as listing additional places where the item has been reviewed. While it is a professional resource, it is not a professional journal. This makes Option D the most appropriate answer.

51. Which of the following is NOT one of three general criteria for selection of all materials?
    (Skill 8.2) Average Rigor

    A. authenticity.
    B. appeal.
    C. appropriateness.
    D. allocation.

Answer: D. allocation

When selecting materials the school library generally looks for materials that have reliable information, appeal to students and are appropriate for the grade levels their program serves. Option D, allocation, is not one of the criteria use to select materials

52. **Which of the following is a book jobber often used by school libraries:**
    (Skill 8.2) Rigorous

    A. Library Media Book Services
    B. Baker and Taylor
    C. Mead and Blackwell
    D. Elementary Book Services

Answer: B. Baker and Taylor

A jobber buys products from a manufacturer and sells it to retailers. One of the more popular book jobbers is Baker and Taylor.

53. **When a new media specialists comes to a library, it is important for them to be come familiar with the existing resource collection. One of the best ways to do this is to:**
    (Skill 8.2) Average rigor

    A. consult the district director regarding collection policies.
    B. browse the shelves to evaluate what is available.
    C. examine collections of other comparable schools.
    D. study the school's curriculum to understand the needs of users.

Answer: B. browse the shelves to evaluate what is available

The most effective way for a media specialist to get to know their media collection is to browse the shelves. The other options may be helpful in determining the overall media program. Option B is the most appropriate answer.

54. **The role of the Media Committee or Media Advisory Committee is to assist with all of the following except:**
    (Skill 8.3) Average rigor

    A. determine program direction
    B. evaluate the media specialist
    C. direct budget decisions
    D. collaborate with the media specialist

Answer: B. evaluate the media specialist

The Media Advisory Committee has the responsibility of helping to determine essential elements of the media collection, but they do not evaluate the media specialist.

55. The process of discarding worn or outdated books and materials is known as:
    (Skill 8.4) Easy

    A. weeding
    B. inventory
    C. collection mapping
    D. eliminating

Answer: A. weeding

Option A is the most appropriate answer. Outdated or worn books and materials need to be removed from the library collection. This process is known as weeding.

56. The practice of examining the quantity and quality of the school library media resource collection which provides a "snapshot" of the collection is called:
    (Skill 8.4) Easy

    A. collection development
    B. collection maintenance
    C. collection mapping
    D. weeding

Answer: C. collection mapping

Collection maps are of great benefit to the school library media specialist. They help to identify strengths and weaknesses in the collection, plan for purchases and identify areas in need of weeding. Option C is the most appropriate answer.

57. Which of these Dewey Decimal classifications should be weeded most often?
    (Skill 8.4) Rigorous

    A. 100s
    B. 500s
    C. 700s
    D. Biographies

Answer: B. 500s

Materials in this section need to be continuously checked to ensure that the scientific information is correct. The 100s should be weeded every five to eight years. The 700s should be kept until worn and biographies keep the most current versions.

58. **Which periodical contains book reviews of currently published children and young adult books?**
    (Skill 8.5) Rigorous

    A. *Phi Delta Kappan*
    B. *School Library Journal*
    C. *School Library Media Quarterly*
    D. *American Teacher*

Answer: B. *School Library Journal*

The *School Library Journal* is the world's largest book review source making Option B the best answer. *Phi Delta Kappan* is a professional journal for education. *School Library Media Quarterly* is a journal published by the American Library Association to assist with program administration of school library media programs. *American Teacher* is a magazine for the teaching profession.

59. **To obtain a clear picture of the library media collection the media specialist can:**
    (Skill 8.6) Easy

    A. Read through the card catalog
    B. conduct a collection analysis
    C. ask teachers for their opinions
    D. none of the above

Answer: B. conduct a collection analysis

Part of a collection analysis involves reading through the collection. Other parts include physically browsing the collection, pull books prior to specific copyright dates, and surveying staff and students to determine resource needs.

60. When selecting books for students in grades k-2, it is best to choose books with which of the following characteristics?
    (Skill 9.1) Easy

    A. strong picture support
    B. familiar language patterns
    C. utilize cuing systems
    D. all of the above

Answer: D. all of the above

The best answer is Option D. Young readers need books that have strong picture support, repetitive language patterns, and strong cuing systems.

61. The creators of the Big 6 Model are:
    (Skill 9.2) Average Rigor

    A. Eisenberg and Berkowitz.
    B. Marzano and Bloom.
    C. Bloom and Gardner.
    D. Lance and Eisenberg.

Answer: A. Eisenberg and Berkowitz

The correct answer is Option A. Mike Eisenberg and Bob Berkowitz are the creators of the Big 6 Model for developing Information Literacy Skills.

62. Steps in the Big6 Model include all of the following except:
    (Skill 9.2) Rigorous

    A. information seeking strategies
    B. location and access
    C. creation of information
    D. task definition

Answer: C. creation of information

Creation of information is the only option that is not included in the Big6 Information Literacy model. Option C is the most appropriate answer.

63. **Skills that provide students with the ability to solve problems are known as**
 (Skill 9.3) Average rigor

 A. critical thinking skills
 B. multiple intelligences
 C. Loertscher's Taxonomies
 D. authentic learning

Answer: A. critical thinking skills

Critical thinking skills are the skills students need to find solutions to complex problems. This makes Option A the most appropriate answer.

64. **Students with disabilities would benefit from specialized software that can read online text, PDF documents and scanned pages. One popular software title is called:**
 (Skill 9.4) Rigorous

 A. Kurzweil Reader
 B. Accelerated Reader
 C. Star Reader
 D. Kertfeld Reader

Answer: A. Kurzweil Reader

The Kurzweil Reader is software that assists students with disabilities. The software can read pdf documents and text online and scanned documents. It is a powerful tool for all students, not just those with disabilities.

65. The TAXONOMIES OF THE SCHOOL LIBRARY MEDIA PROGRAM outlines eleven levels of school library media specialists' involvement with curriculum and instruction and was developed by: *(Skill 9.5) Rigorous*

    A. Eisenberg.
    B. Bloom.
    C. Loertscher.
    D. Lance.

Answer: C. Loertscher

Eisenberg is one of the creators of the Big 6 Model. Bloom was the developer of Bloom's Taxonomy. Keith Curry-Lance has conducted many studies on the effect of school library media programs on student achievement.

66. All of the following organizations serve school libraries except: *(Skill 9.6) Average Rigor*

    A. AASL
    B. AECT
    C. ALCT
    D. ALA

Answer: C. ALCT

The American Association of School Librarians (AASL), The Association for Educational Communications and Technology (AECT), and the American Library Association (ALA) are all organizations that support and serve school libraries.

67. Which of the following is true about essential questions? *(Skill 10.1) Easy*

    A. They are created by teachers to ensure they focus on curricular requirements.
    B. They are at the top of the Loertscher's Taxonomies.
    C. They are open-ended and focus on a broad topic.
    D. They should influence student thought.

Answer: C. They are open-ended and focus on a broad topic

Essential questions are open-ended, are centered around a curricular unit, review curricular standards, and are phrased so that they don't influence student thought.

68. When evaluating resources for effectiveness it is important to consider all of the following except:
    (Skill 10.2) Average Rigor

    A. style of the web page.
    B. the intended audience.
    C. whether or not the site is from a scholarly source.
    D. the scope of the information

Answer: A. Style of the web page.

The style of the web page is not as important as the audience, whether or not the site is a scholarly source, or the scope of the information. This makes Option A the most appropriate answer.

69. A periodical index search which allows the user to pair Keywords with <u>and</u>, <u>but</u>, or <u>or</u> is called
    (Skill 10.3) Average Rigor

    A. Boolean.
    B. dialoguing.
    C. wildcarding.
    D. truncation.

Answer: A. Boolean

The most appropriate answer is Option A, Boolean. A Boolean search uses keywords along with terms such as and, but, and or, to define the search. Wildcarding is a form of searching that uses something such as an asterisks to find different formats of words or terms.

70. A request from a social studies teacher for the creation of a list of historical fiction titles for a book report assignment is a _____ request.
    (Skill 10.4) Rigorous

    A. ready reference.
    B. research.
    C. specific needs.
    D. complex search.

Answer: C. specific needs.

Requests made for particular titles or resources are known as a special needs request. Option C is the most appropriate answer.

71. A search that uses specific terms to locate information is called a:
    (Skill 11.1) Average rigor

    A. reference search
    B. keyword search
    C. ready reference search
    D. operator search

Answer: B. keyword search

A keyword search uses specific terms to locate information. The most appropriate answer is Option B.

72. A catalog that contains materials from several library collections is known as a
    (Skill 11.2) Average rigor

    A. Shared Catalog.
    B. Cooperative Catalog.
    C. Union Catalog.
    D. Universal Catalog.

Answer: C. Union Catalog

Option C is the most appropriate answer. A union catalog exists when various entities combine their resource lists so that they can be shown in one catalog. This is most often done throughout school districts or through partnerships with colleges and universities.

73. Which of the following searches would most likely return the most results?
    (Skill 11.3) Average Rigor

    A. lions and tigers
    B. lions not tigers
    C. lions or tigers
    D. lions and not tigers

Answer: C. Lions or tigers.

The use of OR in the search lets the search engine know to find articles that contain either of the words listed. With the use of AND, the search engine will look for articles that have both words in the article.

LIBRARY & MEDIA SPECIALIST

74. The media specialist is searching a database and needs to locate all of the entries that begin with the letter "P". What is the best way to format this search?
(Skill *11.4*) Average rigor

   A. Create a search using the Boolean operator AND NOT. (P AND NOT A, B, C, D, E...)
   B. Place quotations around the letter P
   C. Use a wildcard
   D. This type of search cannot be done.

Answer: C. Use a wildcard

This is an effective tool if one is unsure of the spelling or date for the topic being searched. . One way to phrase the search is to type P* . The asterisk at the end will cause the search to return anything in the database that begins with the letters "P".

75. A keyword search returns too many results with few relevant records. What does the patron need to do?
(Skill *12.2*) Easy

   A. narrow the search topic
   B. broaden the search topic
   C. find a new topic
   D. none of the above

Answer: A. narrow the search topic

When a keyword search returns too many records or irrelevant records then the patron needs to narrow the search topic. For instance, if the patron is searching for information on German Shepard dogs it would be best to type in that specific phrase instead of just the word "dogs". Option A is the most appropriate answer.

76. A group of students in the business club will be creating a website to sell their product. When selecting their domain name, which of the following extensions would be best to use?
(Skill 12.3) Rigorous

    A. .com
    B. .edu
    C. .cfm
    D. .html

Answer: A. .com

A website that is used for commercial purposes should have a .com extension. The domain name is the location where the web page information is stored. Because the question specifically stated the domain name, Option A is the most appropriate answer. The .edu extension is used for educational institutions. The .html extension refers to the programming used to create a web page and stands for hypertext mark-up language.

77. A kindergarten class has just viewed a video on alligators. The best way to evaluate the suitability of the material for this age group is to (Skill 12.4) Rigorous

    A. test the students' ability to recall the main points of the video.
    B. compare this product to other similar products on this content.
    C. observe the body language and verbal comments during the viewing.
    D. ask the children to comment on the quality of the video at the end of the viewing.

Answer: C. observe the body language and verbal comments during the viewing

Students may be able to view any video and be able to recall facts, but suitability for a particular age may best be evaluated by how well students respond to the video as it is being viewed. This makes Option C the most appropriate answer.

78. **In most learning hierarchies, which of the following is the highest order critical thinking skill?**
    (Skill 12.5) Average Rigor

    A. appreciation.
    B. inference.
    C. recall.
    D. comprehension.

Answer: A. appreciation

In order of difficulty recall is the lowest critical thinking skill, followed by inference then comprehension and appreciation. Appreciation would be the highest level skill in this list, making Option A the most appropriate answer.

79. **After reading *The Pearl*, a tenth grader asks, "Why can't we start sentences with *and* like John Steinbeck?" This student is showing the ability to**
    (Skill 12.5) Rigorous

    A. appreciate.
    B. comprehend.
    C. infer.
    D. evaluate.

Answer: D. evaluate.

Under the description of the Bloom's Taxonomy level of evaluation students that demonstrate this level of higher order thinking are able to :
- Make choices based upon well thought out arguments
- Compare ideas
- And recognize subjectivity

80. A scoring guide that is generally subject and contains specific criteria in which projects should be judged is known as a:
    (Skill 12.6) Easy

    A. rubric
    B. outline
    C. criteria
    D. evaluation

Answer: A. rubric

Rubrics are popular grading scales that can be used for product based assessments. Rubrics generally provide criteria that is based on a specific rating scale. Grades are determined by how closely the student has met the criteria.

81. All but which of the following criteria are used when determining fair use of copyrighted material for classroom use?
    (Skill 13.1) Average Rigor

    A. Brevity Test.
    B. Spontaneity Test.
    C. Time Test.
    D. Cumulative Effect Test.

Answer: C. Time Test

Copyrighted materials used in a classroom must pass the criteria under the brevity, spontaneity, and cumulative effect tests in order to fall under the fair use guidelines.

82. Section 108 of the Copyright Act permits the copying of an entire book if three conditions are met. Which of the following is NOT one of those conditions?
    (Skill 13.1) Rigorous

    A. The library intends to allow inter- library loan of the book.
    B. The library is an archival library.
    C. The copyright notice appears on all the copies.
    D. The library is a public library.

Answer: A. The library intends to allow inter-library loan of the book.

Section 108 does allow a library to make a single copy of a book for archival purposes. It does not cover books that are to be copied and used for inter-library loans.

83. Under the copyright brevity test, an educator may reproduce without written permission
    (Skill 13.1) Rigorous

    A. 10% of any prose or poetry work.
    B. 500 words from a 5000 word article.
    C. 240 words of a 2400 word story.
    D. no work over 2500 words.

Answer: B. 500 words from a 5000 word article.

Under the brevity test up to 250 words of a poem can be copied providing it is under 2 pages. An article of 2500 words or less can be copied entirely. Ten percent of an article over 2500 words can be used making Option B the most appropriate answer.

84. Licensing has become a popular means of copyright protection in the area of
(Skill 13.1) Average Rigor

    A. duplicating books for interlibrary loan.
    B. use of software application on multiple machines.
    C. music copying.
    D. making transparency copies of books or workbooks that are too expensive to purchase.

Answer: B. Use of software application on multiple machines.

When purchasing software the customer will generally received either a CD-ROM or DVD for installation purposes. The most important piece of packaging or file included on the software is the license. The license(s) purchased determine the number of computers in which the software can be loaded. Installing the software on more than the number listed on the license violated copyright and can result in a lawsuit by the publisher.

85. "Fair Use" policy in videotaping off-air from commercial television requires
(Skill 13.1) Rigorous

    A. show in 5 days, erase by the 20th day.
    B. show in 10 days, erase by the 30th day.
    C. show in 10 days, erase by the 45th day.
    D. no restrictions.

Answer: C. Show in 10 days, erase by the 45th day.

Fair Use Guidelines for recorded videotapes for nonprofit educational institutions state that the recording must be shown within 10 days and must be erased by the 45th day.

86. **MLA style is a popular format for citing resources in a bibliography. MLA is the acronym for:**
    (Skill 13.2) Rigorous

    A. Media Library Association
    B. Modern Library Association
    C. Modern Literary Association
    D. Modern Language Association

Answer: D. Modern Language Association

MLA format is a popular format for citing resources. The acronym stands for Modern Language Association.

87. **When creating instructional materials which of the following is not a part of the planning phase?**
    (Skill 13.3) Rigorous

    A. determining the goal or objectives to be covered
    B. create the media
    C. analyze the audience
    D. determine the purpose

Answer: B. create the media

Creating the media is part of the design phase while the others are key parts of the planning phase.

88. **Which of the following formats is best for large group presentations?**
    (Skill 13.4) Easy

    A. manipulatives
    B. multimedia
    C. audio recordings
    D. photographs

Answer: B. multimedia

Multimedia presentations are most appropriate for large groups. When used in conjunction with projectors and large screens, multimedia presentations are very effective.

89. All of the following formats are best for small group learning except:
    (Skill 13.4) Average rigor

    A. manipulatives
    B. computer projection
    C. photographs
    D. computer software

Answer: D. computer software

Computer software used on a single machine is most appropriate for small groups. The most appropriate answer is Option D.

90. An elementary teacher, planning a unit on the local environment, finds materials that are too global or above her students' ability level. The best solution to this problem is to
    (Skill 13.5) Average rigor

    A. broaden the scope of the study to emphasize global concerns.
    B. eliminate the unit from the content.
    C. replace the unit with another unit that teaches the same skills.
    D. have the students design their own study materials using media production techniques.

Answer: D. have the students design their own study materials using media production techniques.

When commercial materials cannot be found to meet student needs, the best alternative is to have students design their own materials. By designing and creating their own materials students tend to develop a deeper understanding of the material.

91. The most effective method of initiating closer contacts with and determining the needs of classroom teachers is to
    (Skill 14.1) Average Rigor

    A. ask to be included on the agenda of periodic faculty meetings.
    B. present after school or weekend in-services in opening communication channels.
    C. request permission to be included in grade-level or content-area meetings.
    D. establish a library advisory committee with one representative from each grade level or content area.

Answer: C. Request permission to be included in grade-level or content-area meetings.

Collaboration is a key component of any successful school library media program. By participating in grade level or content area meetings the media specialist can get a better idea of the specific needs of teachers

92. This outlines the role of the school library media specialist and the programs they manage.
    (Skill 14.2) Rigorous

    A. Taxonomies of Learning
    B. Code of Ethics
    C. @ Your Library
    D. Library Bill of Rights

Answer: C. @ Your Library

As part of ALA's Advocacy Toolkit, @ Your Library outlines the role of the school library media specialist and the programs they manage. This makes Option C the most appropriate response.

93. Which of the following is not a benefit of forming partnerships within the community?
   (Skill 14.3) Average rigor

   A. increased support for media program
   B. decline in media resources
   C. provide wide array of resources
   D. increase parental involvement

Answer: B. decline in media resources

By forming partnerships with outside agencies the media specialist can often increase the resources available for their patrons. Option B is the most appropriate answer because forming partnerships does not decrease media resources.

94. Which of the following is NOT an expert in child development?
   (Skill 14.4) Rigorous

   A. Lawrence Kohlberg.
   B. James Naisbitt.
   C. Jean Piaget.
   D. Erik Erikson.

Answer: B. James Naisbitt

Kohlberg is the developer of Modes of Learning. Piaget is one of the most influential developmental psychologists. Erik Erikson is also a well-known developmental psychologists. James Naisbitt is an author in the field of future studies making him the only one not involved in child development and Option B the best answer.

95. Contemporary library media design models should consider which of the following an optional need?
    (Skill 15.1) Rigorous

    A. flexibility of space to allow for reading, viewing, and listening.
    B. space for large group activities such as district meetings, standardized testing, and lectures.
    C. traffic flow patterns for entrance and exit from the media center as well as easy movement within the center.
    D. adequate and easy to rearrange storage areas for the variety of media formats and packaging style of modern materials.

Answer: B. space for large group activities such as district meetings, standardized testing, and lectures.

Flexibility of space, traffic flow patterns that allow ease of movement, and adequate storage are all crucial to design of a media center. Therefore, Option B is the best answer. While a space for large group activities is desirable for community use, it is not vital to the operation of a school library media center.

96. Key design elements to consider when renovating or building a new facility include:
    (Skill 15.1) Average rigor

    A. Traffic flow
    B. Access for physically impaired users
    C. Security needs
    D. all of the above

Answer: D. all of the above

Whether planning for a new media center or renovating an existing one there are many things that need to be taken into consideration. Among the considerations are the traffic flow, plans for access for impaired users and security. Other considerations would be appropriate space for specific tasks and furniture height. This makes Option D the most appropriate answer.

97. **When automating a library catalog it is important to consider which of the following prior to set up?**
    (Skill 15.2) Average rigor

    A. technical requirements
    B. loan period
    C. patron limitations
    D. color of spine labels

Answer: A. technical requirements

Prior to establishing or upgrading an automated library catalog one of the most important considerations should be the technical requirements. Schools should examine their network infrastructure and individual computers to determine if it will support the systems.

98. ***Information Power: Building Partnerships for Learning* recommends flexible scheduling for**
    (Skill 15.3) Easy

    A. elementary school library media centers.
    B. middle school library media centers.
    C. secondary school library media centers.
    D. all school library media centers.

Answer: D. all school library media centers.

Flexible access to resources is conducive to encouraging just-in-time learning. Resources are available at the point of need. Collaboration with classroom teachers makes flexible access even more effective. Thus all of the school library media centers should follow a flexible schedule making Option D the most appropriate answer

99. When creating a schedule for a school library media center the type of schedule that maximizes access to resources is a:
    (Skill 15.3) Easy

    A. fixed schedule
    B. open schedule
    C. partial fixed schedule
    D. flexible schedule

Answer: D. flexible schedule

The best answer is d, flexible schedule. A flexible schedule allows students to have access to resources at the point of need. It maximizes the use of resources and allows media specialists to be accessible for collaborative planning with teachers.

100. The procedures for conducting an inventory of the media collection include all of the following except:
     (Skill 15.4) Rigorous

     A. Determine the cost of the inventory.
     B. Determine when the inventory will be conducted.
     C. Determine who will conduct the inventory.
     D. Determine if each item matches the information in the holding records.

Answer: A. Determine the cost of the inventory.

When conducting an inventory it is not necessary to determine the cost of the inventory. Option A is the most appropriate answer.

101. The Library Bill of Rights includes all of the following except:
    (Skill 15.5) Rigorous

    A. Information presented in a library should be selected based upon the age level of the students.
    B. Resources should include a representation of all ideas, concepts, and backgrounds.
    C. Resources should not be excluded because of viewpoint.
    D. Censorship should be challenged.

Answer: A. Information presented in a library should be selected based upon the age level of the students.

Libraries should work to provide as much access to resources as possible. Resources should not be selected solely based upon age level of students. This makes Option A the most appropriate answer.

102. In which bibliographic field should information concerning the format of an audio-visual material appear?
    (Skill 16.1) Rigorous

    A. Material specific details.
    B. Physical description.
    C. Notes.
    D. Standard numbers.

Answer: C. Notes

Using the 500 – General Note field in a MARC record the format of the audio-visual materials can be listed. This makes Option C the most appropriate answer. The physical description contains information about the price and number of pages.

103. MARC is the acronym for:
    (Skill 16.1) Easy

    A. Mobile Accessible Recorded Content
    B. Machine Accessible Readable Content
    C. Machine Readable Content
    D. Mobile Accessible Readable Content

Answer: C. Machine Readable Content

Option C is the most appropriate answer. MARC is the acronym for Machine Readable Content. The MARC format is used in the cataloging of resources.

104. **AACR2 is the acronym for:**
    (Skill 16.1) Easy

    A. Anglo-American Cataloging Rules Second Edition
    B. American Association of Cataloging Rules Second Edition
    C. American Association of Content Rules Second Edition
    D. Anglo-American Content Rules Second Edition

Answer: A. Anglo-American Cataloging Rules Second Edition

Option A is the most appropriate answer. AACR2 outlines specific rules that must be followed when cataloging items.

105. **OCLC is the acronym for:**
    (Skill 16.1) Average rigor

    A. Online Computer Library Center
    B. Online Computer Library Catalog
    C. Online Computer Library Conference
    D. Online Computer Library Content

Answer: A. Online Computer Library Center

The most appropriate answer is Option A, the Online Computer Library Center. This center provides bibliographic (MARC) records.

106. **In MARC records the title information can be found under which tag?**
    (Skill 16.1) Rigorous

    A. 130
    B. 245
    C. 425
    D. 520

Answer: B. 245

The 245 tag is where the title information is recorded in a MARC record. Option B is the most appropriate response. The 520 tag is where the summary is listed.

TEACHER CERTIFICATION STUDY GUIDE

107. Collection development policies are developed to accomplish all of the following except
    (Skill 16.1) Rigorous

    A. guarantee users freedom to access information.
    B. recognize the needs and interests of users.
    C. coordinate selection criteria and budget concerns.
    D. recognize rights of individuals or groups to challenge these policies.

Answer: C. coordinate selection criteria and budget concerns

The main goal of a collection development policy is to set guidelines and procedures that govern how resources are purchased and managed. It does not coordinate any criteria or address funding issues.

108. All of the following are components of a circulation policy except:
    (Skill 16.4) Rigorous

    A. loan period
    B. process for handling overdues
    C. limitations
    D. location to post borrower's name

Answer: D. location to post borrower's name

The location to post a borrower's name is not a part of a circulation policy. The policy should include the length of the loan period, how to handle overdues, and such limitations as the number of books that can be checked out at once.

109. Ongoing evaluation is necessary to produce a quality media program. Use of evaluation results be used for all of the following except:
    (Skill 16.5) Easy

    A. lobbying for budgetary or personnel support
    B. to make changes to the use of the media center materials
    C to determine circulation regulations
    D. all of the above

Answer: D. all of the above

Evaluating a media program can be very beneficial. It can assist the media specialist in justifying budget requests, making changes to the media center resources, and determine circulation regulations. Option D is the most appropriate answer.

110. **Which of the following are examples of ways to promote the school library media programs:**
    (Skill 17.2) Easy

    A. Attend school board meetings
    B. Serve on the school's curriculum committee
    C. Invite school board members to media planning meetings
    D. All of the above

Answer: D. All of the above

Option D is the most appropriate answer. To promote the school library media program it is important that the media specialist attend school board meetings, serve on the school's curriculum committee and invite school board members and other officials to media planning meetings.

111. **In formulating an estimated collection budget consider all of the following except**
    (Skill 17.3) Rigorous

    A. attrition by loss, damage, or age.
    B. the maximum cost of item replacement.
    C. the number of students served.
    D. the need for expansion to meet minimum guidelines.

Answer: B. the maximum cost of item replacement

The first consideration for formulating a collection budget is to determine whether or not the collection meets minimum guidelines. Then decide upon the funding needed to meet the guidelines. It is also important to allot funds to replace lost or worn items. Option B, the maximum cost of item replacement is not used in formulating a collection budget making it the most appropriate answer.

112. The most appropriate means of obtaining extra funds for library media programs is
    (Skill 17.4) Average Rigor

    A. having candy sales.
    B. conducting book fairs.
    C. charging fines.
    D. soliciting donations.

Answer: B. conducting book fairs.

The most appropriate answer for this question is Option B, conducting book fairs. This keeps in line with the main focus of a school library media program, literacy.

113. A school with 500 – 749 students should have how many media specialists?
    (Skill 17.5) Easy

    A. 1 part-time media specialist
    B. 1 full time media specialist
    C. 2 full time media specialist
    D. no media specialist required

Answer: B. 1 full time media specialist

It is recommended that schools with 500 to 749 students have at least 1 full time media specialist. This makes Option B the most appropriate response.

114. The most efficient method of evaluating support staff is to
    (Skill 17.6) Average Rigor

    A. administer a written test.
    B. survey faculty whom they serve.
    C. observe their performance.
    D. obtain verbal confirmation during an employee interview.

Answer: C. observe their performance

The most efficient method of evaluating support staff is to observe their performance. An observation can provide an overall picture of the tasks they routinely perform. Observations may be conducted by the media specialist alone or in conjunction with another school administrator or fellow media specialist.

115. Which of the following is an example of quantitative data that would be used to evaluate a school library media program?
    (Skill 18.1) Average rigor

    A. Personnel evaluations
    B. Usage statistics
    C. Surveys
    D. Interviews

Answer: B. Usage statistics

Option B is the most appropriate answer because it is the only one listed that provides measurable data. All of the others are qualitative forms of data.

116. An accredited elementary school has maintained an acceptable number of items in its print collection for ten years. In the evaluation review, this fact is evidence of both
    (Skill 18.1) Rigorous

    A. diagnostic and projective standards.
    B. diagnostic and quantitative standards.
    C. projective and quantitative standards.
    D. projective and qualitative standards.

Answer: B. diagnostic and quantitative standards.

Diagnostic evaluations are standards based on conditions existing in programs that have already been judged excellent. The acceptable print collection can be compared to national guidelines for diagnostic information. Quantitative evaluations involve numerical data of some kind. By taking a look at the numbers in the collection the media specialist can review collection totals.

TEACHER CERTIFICATION STUDY GUIDE

117. The principal is completing the annual report. He needs to include substantive data on use of the media center. In addition to the number of book circulations, he would like to know the proportionate use of the media center's facilities and services by the various grade levels or content areas. This information can most quickly be obtained from:
    (Skill 18.1) Rigorous

    A. the class scheduling log.
    B. student surveys.
    C. lesson plans.
    D. inventory figures.

Answer: A. the class scheduling log

One of the best tools to use to determine how the media center's facilities are being used is the schedule. Often the schedule is broken down by the various areas in the media center. Teachers may schedule the specific area(s) they need. This makes Option A the most appropriate answer.

118. A general statement or outcome that is broken down into specific skills. This statement is known as a:
    (Skill 18.2) Average rigor

    A. policy
    B. procedure
    C. goal
    D. objective

Answer: C. goal

A goal is a general statement or outcome that is broken down into specific measurable objectives. Option C is the most appropriate answer.

119. **A statement defining the core principles of a school library media program is called the:**
    (Skill 18.2) Average Rigor

    A. mission
    B. policy
    C. procedure
    D. objective

Answer: A. mission

The core principles of an organization are outlined in a mission statement. An objective is a specific statement of measurable result that reflects the mission statement.

120. **Which of the following is a library policy, not a procedure?**
    (Skill 18.2) Rigorous

    A. providing a vehicle for the circulation of audio-visual equipment.
    B. setting guidelines for collection development.
    C. determining the method for introducing an objective into the school improvement plan.
    D. setting categorical limits on operating expenses.

Answer: B. setting guidelines for collection development.

A policy is a plan or a course of action such as setting the guidelines for collection development as listed in Option B. A procedure is a set of specific steps or methods used to perform a specific action.

121. **A procedure is:**
    (Skill 18.2) Easy

    A. a course of action taken to execute a plan.
    B. a written statement of principle used to guarantee a management practice.
    C. a statement of core values of an organization.
    D. a regulation concerning certification.

Answer: A. a course of action taken to execute a plan.

The most appropriate answer was Option A. A procedure is a course of action taken to execute a plan. A mission is a statement of core values.

122. Long range plans should span how many years?
 (Skill 18.3) Easy

   A. 2 – 4
   B. 3 – 5
   C. 5 – 10
   D. 10 – 15

Answer: B. 3-5

Long range plans should be developed to span from 3-5 years. It is important to record progress and plan periodic evaluations to determine which goals may need to be adjusted due to changing student populations and funding.

123. Ongoing evaluation is necessary to produce a quality media program. Use of evaluation results be used for all of the following except:
 (Skill 18.4) Rigorous

   A. lobbying for budgetary or personnel support
   B. to make changes to the use of the media center materials
   C. to determine circulation regulations
   D. all of the above

Answer: D. all of the above

Evaluating a media program can be very beneficial. It can assist the media specialist in justifying budget requests, making changes to the media center resources, and determine circulation regulations. Option D is the most appropriate answer.

124. Parent involvement is critical to the support of a school and media program. Which of the following is the least effective way to increase parent involvement:
    (Skill 7.5) Easy

    A. Plan special family nights.
    B. Plan parent workshops
    C. Involve parents as volunteers.
    D. Send notes home to parents

Answer: D. Send notes home to parents

Sending notes home is not as effective as actually involving parents in school activities. Option D is the most appropriate answer.

125. For students to take responsibility for their own learning the media specialist much teach them all of the following but:
    (Skill 1.6) Easy

    A. locate resources.
    B. evaluate resources.
    C. purchase resources
    D. use resources.

Answer: C. purchase resources

For students to be information literate they should know how to find, evaluation and use resources. It is not necessary for students to know to purchase materials.

XAMonline, INC. 21 Orient Ave. Melrose, MA 02176

Toll Free number 800-509-4128

TO ORDER Fax 781-662-9268 OR www.XAMonline.com

NEW YORK STATE TEACHER CERTIFICATION EXAMINATION - NYSTCE - 2007

PO#   Store/School:

Address 1:

Address 2 (Ship to other):

City, State Zip

Credit card number _____-_____-_____-_____   expiration_____

EMAIL _____

PHONE   FAX

13# ISBN 2007	TITLE	Qty	Retail	Total
978-1-58197-866-7	NYSTCE ATS-W ASSESSMENT OF TEACHING SKILLS- WRITTEN 91			
978-1-58197-867-4	NYSTCE ATAS ASSESSMENT OF TEACHING ASSISTANT SKILLS 095			
978-1-58197-854-4	CST BIOLOGY 006			
978-1-58197-855-1	CST CHEMISTRY 007			
978-1-58197-865-0	CQST COMMUNICATION AND QUANTITATIVE SKILLS TEST 080			
978-1-58197-856-8	CST EARTH SCIENCE 008			
978-1-58197-851-3	CST ENGLISH 003			
978-1-58197-862-9	CST FAMILY AND CONSUMER SCIENCES 072			
978-1-58197-858-2	CST FRENCH SAMPLE TEST 012			
978-1-58197-868-1	LAST LIBERAL ARTS AND SCIENCE TEST 001			
978-1-58197-863-6	CST LIBRARY MEDIA SPECIALIST 074			
978-1-58197-861-2	CST LITERACY 065			
978-1-58197-852-0	CST MATH 004			
978-1-58197-872-8	CST MULTIPLE SUBJECTS 002 SAMPLE QUESTIONS			
978-1-58197-850-6	CST MUTIPLE SUBJECTS 002			
978-1-58197-864-3	CST PHYSICAL EDUCATION 076			
978-1-58197-857-5	CST PHYSICS SAMPLE TEST 009			
978-1-58197-853-7	CST SOCIAL STUDIES 005			
978-1-58197-859-9	CST SPANISH 020			
978-1-58197-860-5	CST STUDENTS WITH DISABILITIES 060			
			SUBTOTAL	
	FOR PRODUCT PRICES VISIT WWW.XAMONLINE.COM		Ship	$8.25
			TOTAL	

www.ingramcontent.com/pod-product-compliance
Lightning Source LLC
Chambersburg PA
CBHW080540300426
44111CB00017B/2807